OBSERVE
INTERPRET
APPLY

HANS FINZEL
WITH PATRICIA H. PICARDI

A DIVISION OF SCRIPTURE PRESS PUBLICATIONS INC.
USA CANADA ENGLAND

Unless otherwise indicated, Scripture quotations are from the *Holy Bible, New International Version* ®. Copyright © 1973, 1978, 1984 by International Bible Society. Used by permission of Zondervan Publishing House. All rights reserved. Other quotations are from *New American Standard Bible* (NASB), © the Lockman Foundation 1960, 1962, 1963, 1968, 1971, 1972, 1973, 1975, 1977; *New Revised Standard Version* (NRSV), © 1989, by the Division of Christian Education of the National Council of Churches of Christ in the U.S.A. All rights reserved.

Portions of this book previously appeared in *Unlocking the Scriptures*, Hans Finzel, © 1986 by SP Publications and in *Opening the Book, Hans Finzel,* © 1987 by SP Publications. Used by permission.

Editor: Carolyn Nystrom
Cover Design: Joe DeLeon
Cover Illustration: Frank McShane,
  represented by Creative Freelancers

Library of Congress Cataloging-in-Publication Data

Finzel, Hans.
  Observe, interpret, apply: how to study the Bible inductively/by Hans Finzel.
    p.   cm.
    ISBN 1-56476-221-1
    1. Bible—Study and teaching. I. Title. II. Title: Study the Bible inductively.
BS600.2.F54 1994
220'.07—dc20   93-50742
                                                                              CIP

1   2   3   4   5   6   7   8   9   10   Printing/Year   98   97   96   95   94

© 1994 by Victor Books/SP Publications, Inc. All rights reserved. Printed in the United States of America. No part of this book may be reproduced without written permission, except for brief quotations in books, critical articles, and reviews.

VICTOR BOOKS
A division of SP Publications, Inc.
1825 College Avenue, Wheaton, Illinois 60187

CONTENTS

Foreword 5
Author's Note 7
1. The Bible and You 9
2. What Is Inductive Bible Study? 13

PART ONE

3. *Step 1: Observation* Asks, "What Do I See?" 19
4. Looking at the Whole 28
5. Looking at the Parts 33
6. Looking at the Details 41
7. *Step 2: Interpretation* Asks, "What Does It Mean?" 46
8. The How To's of Interpretation 53
9. *Step 3: Application* Asks, "How Should I Respond?" 66
10. In Application, God's Word Studies Us 72

PART TWO

11. How to Study a Whole Book of the Bible 81
12. *Narratives* — True Stories about God and His People 85
13. *Epistles* — Letters with a Purpose 107
14. *Wisdom Literature* and *Poetry* — Truths to Remember 128
15. *Prophecy* and *Revelation* — Judgment with Hope 152
16. How to Study a Topic 174
17. How to Study a Person 194
18. How to Study Key Words 199
19. How to Study a Doctrine 205

Personal Evaluation 210

Group Study Guide 212

Appendix A — Defining Bible Study Aids 231
Appendix B — Bible Study Resource List 232
Appendix C — Principles of Structure 235

Notes 239

Summary Sheet 241

FOREWORD

Personal Bible study is the Christian's lifeline. It is never optional; always essential. When Paul urged his protegé Timothy, "Do your best to present yourselves to God as one approved, a workman who does not need to be ashamed and who correctly handles the word of truth" (2 Timothy 2:15, NIV), he underscored the essential nature of the Scriptures in fostering quality spiritual living.

Hans Finzel has served the body well in providing a practical guide for studying the Word for oneself. Too many believers are under the Word but not personally in it.

The model he presents is both workable and realistic. It has been tested in a variety of settings and with varied groups of people, including cross-cultural involvement.

It is a delight to commend the work of a colleague to anyone seriously interested in developing the skill of firsthand Bible study. It will change your life!

Howard G. Hendricks
Distinguished Professor
Chairman, Center for Christian Leadership
Dallas Theological Seminary

AUTHOR'S NOTE

This book is for people who want to seriously study the Bible for themselves. There is a tremendous need today to train Christians to understand Scripture and apply it to their lives. At a time when society is increasingly challenging the relevancy of the Bible, it is my hope that this book will bring the joy of discovery back into your study of Scripture.

What makes this book different from other books that teach you how to study the Bible? All too often, "how to" books on Bible study focus on the theoretical and never address how to interpret and apply what's been taught. Conversely, some other books speak of nonstop contemporary application, but they never get around to examining a biblical text. This book breaks down concepts into logical steps of understanding *and* action. As students of Scripture, our goal in studying the Bible is to become more like Christ—to be "*doers* of the *Word*."

Not only does this book take a fresh approach to Bible study, but it presents a practical way of learning Scripture. This is a *work*book. Each step of the way you'll find opportunities to practice what has just been presented—right here in the book! By the time you reach the end you will have completed several Bible studies for yourself. With hard work, this hands-on approach will yield a lifetime of fruitful Bible study. The sample studies and "Your Turn" activities throughout the book provide quick references for questions you may have when studying Scripture in the future. There is even a summary sheet of the basic principles in the back. Tear it out and keep it in your Bible as an outline for future studies you do on your own.

The approach of this book is different, but the basic idea is not; the inductive approach is a proven method for studying the Bible. As you practice the three steps of inductive Bible study—*observation, interpretation,* and *application*—you'll begin to understand and apply God's Word in rich and personal ways. Whether you are studying a passage, a specific topic, or an entire book of the Bible, inductive study addresses three questions:

☐ What do I see? *(observation)*
☐ What does it mean? *(interpretation)*
☐ How should I respond? *(application)*

Once you've worked through the chapters of this book, you will probably want to refer to it often. For instance, if you're leading a Bible study on the Book of Ephesians, you might refer to chapter 13 on how to study epistles. Or if you want to do a personal study of one of the stories in Genesis, chapter 12 shows you what to look for in narratives. Are you a pastor or teacher giving a series of sermons on famous Bible characters? Chapter 17 on how to study a person provides important principles and guidelines to keep in mind as you prepare.

God wants us to know Him in a personal and life-changing way. He took on our nature and died in order to offer us forgiveness and restore us to Himself. He has given us His Holy Spirit so that we can always be near Him. He has equipped His church with people who can instruct us in the life of discipleship. And He has revealed Himself in His written Word. Three things, however, are necessary on our part if we are to accurately interpret this Word: a heart submitted to Jesus Christ, time, and a pattern of study. If you are hungry to know God's Word, the tools presented here can be your utensils.

So, roll up your sleeves and let's dig in!

—Hans Finzel
1994

CHAPTER 1
The Bible and You

Studying the message of the Bible transformed my life. Having grown up in the 60s, there was a lot that needed to be transformed! I was in college during the height of the protests against American involvement in Vietnam and against authority in general. I was a part of that protest—not just the revolution of idealists against political wrongdoing—but a revolution against all order and authority. In time, I lost the ability to bring order even to my own life.

Then I met some Christians who told me about Jesus Christ and pointed me to the Bible. I remember thinking: *Here is Someone I can follow.* What happened in my life at that point was a revolution in the deepest sense of the word.

Of all the books ever written, the Bible is unique. It not only contains miracles, it is itself a miracle. The Bible was authored by God but written through ordinary men.

> *Above all, you must understand that no prophecy of Scripture came about by the prophet's own interpretation. For prophecy never had its origin in the will of man, but men spoke from God as they were carried along by the Holy Spirit.*
> —2 Peter 1:20-21

A brief look at the formation and preservation of the Bible throughout history reveals the high priority God has placed on ensuring that His revelation reaches men and women from generation to generation.

The Formation and Preservation of Scripture

The Bible is history's greatest writing project. It was written across three continents (Asia, Europe, and Africa), over a span of 1,500 years, by men of various walks of life, kings, fishermen, poets, shepherds, philosophers, peasants, teachers, statesmen, Jews, Gentiles, even a doctor and a tax collector. The Bible is a collection of sixty-six books (not including the Apocrypha) and, despite the tremendous variety of writers and the length of time represented in its pages, one central message permeates its contents: faith in Jesus Christ alone frees us from our sins.

Throughout history there have been those who loved and those who despised the Bible. From the Roman emperor Diocletian—who in A.D. 303 ordered that all Bibles be burned—down through the Middle Ages and into the persecutions of the nineteenth and twentieth centuries, the Bible has survived. Not only has it survived, it has spread—with portions of it now translated into over 2,224 languages. As the inscription on the monument in Paris to the French Huguenots reads: "Hammer away, ye hostile hands; your hammer breaks; God's anvil stands."

The Bible is still the best-selling book around the world. Men and women from every nation and social background read and study its contents. Why? Because its Author knows the human heart and speaks to the needs of all people everywhere.

Why We Need to Study the Bible

When you take a trip to a place you've never been, you probably refer to a road map to plot a course, get a general sense of the terrain you'll be passing through, and mark your progress along the way. As Christians, we are on a journey of sorts all of our lives; we are earthly pilgrims on our way home to heaven. But since we have never been there, we must trust our sense of direction to the map of Scripture. If we let it, the Bible will guide us, redirect us when we get off the course, and lead us safely to our destination.

There are two fundamental aspects to Bible study. On the one hand, there is a spiritual dimension to study—our condition and relationship to God. On the other hand is the natural dimension—the educational principles that are employed in studying any piece of literature. Careful Bible study takes both aspects into consideration.

The Bible is in part a human book, and therefore there is a natural dimension to Bible study. This workbook is designed to teach those principles that are necessary for gaining knowledge through study. But the Bible is fundamentally a divine book. It is God's revelation, written by men inspired by the Holy Spirit. That is why David prayed, "Open my eyes that I may see wonderful things in Your law" (Psalm 119:18). It is this uniquely divine nature of Scripture that constantly challenges us to submit our own way of thinking and behaving to its teaching.

The Bible and You

As you complete the following exercise, think about the attitudes with which you approach the Bible. These Scripture texts reveal some of the heart conditions which are necessary for meaningful Bible study. Look up each verse and briefly summarize the attitude expressed.

HEART CONDITION IN BIBLE STUDY

Scripture	Attitude
Psalm 119:18	
1 Corinthians 2:6-16	
Hebrews 11:1-2, 6	
James 1:22-25	

When we study the Bible, we can approach it with childlike trust and dependence (Jesus said in Mark 10:13-15 that this is a necessity), knowing that our Heavenly Father desires to reveal His truths to us.

The Goal of Bible Study
People study the Bible for all kinds of reasons. When I was a missionary in Europe, my study of Scripture was the fodder for my ministry. Now as the director of a mission agency, it nurtures my soul. As teachings of the Bible change me, I can be an agent of change—since all genuine ministry flows out of what we are and not what we do.

Personal Bible study requires effort. But like mining for gold or precious gems, the harder and more thoroughly we dig and sift through the material, the more treasures we find. Just as there is no better way to train for a marathon than to regularly run long distances, (in rain as well as sunshine), there is just no substitute for hard work in Bible study. Paul lived out this perspective and encouraged others to be like him. He said, "Do you not know that in a race all the runners run, but only one gets the prize? Run in such a way as to get the prize" (1 Corinthians 9:24).

YOUR TURN

Each Scripture text below illustrates some reasons for studying the Bible. Look up each verse and briefly summarize the motive suggested. These reasons will be helpful to keep in mind whenever you study the Word of God.

BENEFITS OF PERSONAL BIBLE STUDY

Scripture	Personal Benefit
Joshua 1:8	
Psalm 119:9, 11	
Psalm 119:105	
Matthew 4:1-11	
John 15:5-7	
2 Timothy 3:16-17	
1 John 5:13	

PERSONAL GOALS

What are your reasons for working through this book? What do you hope to gain by the end? Here, at the outset of your study, make a list of several goals you hope to achieve. Keep these goals in mind as you study each chapter.

Goal #1: _____

Goal #2: _____

Goal #3: _____

Goal #4: _____

CHAPTER 2
What Is Inductive Bible Study?

Imagine waking up in the middle of the night with terrible pains in your abdomen. Earlier that evening at a friend's home you had a meal that didn't quite agree with you. You suspect that you have a mild case of food poisoning, but you can't be certain without more facts. The next morning you visit your family doctor and tell her, "Doctor, I'm sure it's food poisoning." The physician, familiar with the process of discovering medical truth, begins to study your case by observing all the characteristics of your body, in light of the symptoms you've described. Only after she has all the facts (blood test, x-ray, physical examination) and has carefully studied the results does she draw a conclusion. In this case, she concludes that you have appendicitis, not food poisoning. You need surgery.

The doctor used an inductive approach to diagnose your ailment. The word *inductive* describes reasoning which proceeds from basic facts to conclusions. We will use the inductive approach to study Scripture. Therefore, we won't state our conclusions about the meaning of a passage or book until carefully examining the facts.

The Three Steps of Inductive Bible Study
The inductive approach involves three steps: *observe, interpret, apply.* To illustrate how these three steps work together, let's go back to the example of you and the doctor.

When the doctor examined you, she followed certain steps to understand your condition. She first *observed* everything she could about your symptoms and behavior. She took your temperature, poked at your abdomen, performed tests. She then *interpreted* her findings, concluding that you had appendicitis. Finally, she *applied* her conclusion by prescribing surgery, medication, and rest. These three steps answer the three key questions of Bible study:

- ☐ What do I see? *(observation)*
- ☐ What does it mean? *(interpretation)*
- ☐ How should I respond? *(application)*

Observation asks, "What do I see?" Observation is simply the gathering of all the facts of who, what, where, and when. Careful examination of the facts is the foundation upon which we build accurate interpretation and application of Scripture. The more time spent looking at the text itself, reading and rereading it, the more fruitful our study will be. Chapters 4 through 6 explain and demonstrate the principles of effective observation, pointing out specifically what questions to ask and what information to look for.

Interpretation asks, "What does it mean?" Drawing conclusions based on your study of the facts is the process of interpretation. During this stage we seek to understand the meaning that the author had in mind when he wrote the text. Chapters 7 and 8 present the fundamental principles for making sound interpretations.

Application asks, "How should I respond?" Application is the goal of Bible study. It is not enough for us to understand (interpret) Scripture; God wants us to be changed by it. The Scriptures were given "for reproof, for correction, and for training in righteousness, so that everyone who belongs to God may be proficient, equipped for every good work" (2 Timothy 3:16-17, NRSV). In this final step of the inductive process, we move from the original context to our contemporary one, seeking to know how our interpretation can affect our attitudes and behavior. In the first two stages, observation and interpretation, we study the text; in application, the text studies us. Chapters 9 and 10 provide guidelines for applying Scripture to our lives so that we may be more like Christ.

Part One of this workbook covers the nuts and bolts of how to study the Bible inductively—with many opportunities for practice. Part Two takes this information and experience and tailors it to meet various Bible study goals you may have. The same three steps are used, but particular attention is given to how the different types of literature found in the Bible (like poetry, prophecy, narrative) each require special consideration when studying them. Just as we don't read the newspaper the same way we read a poem, the parables in the Gospels require different considerations than the narrative sections.

You may want to understand the meaning of an entire book of the Bible, or do a detailed study of a small portion of Scripture—perhaps a single paragraph of an epistle, or see what the Bible as a whole says concerning a given topic. You use the same method of *observation, interpretation,* and *application* for all three of these kinds of studies, while bearing in mind the particular genre or literature type you are studying.

How Do You Study Scripture?

There is no end to the wealth of wisdom in the Bible. Discovering the riches of God's truth throughout our lives is the primary reason for using a book like this. By the time you reach the end you will know and have practiced the three-step approach of inductive Bible study so that you can use this approach for personal study of any Scripture.

To introduce the inductive method of Bible study, let's begin with a little self-examination.

YOUR TURN

Read the following passage from Jonah 1 several times. After carefully thinking about what you have read, answer the four questions that follow. If you cannot answer a question, go on to the next one. This exercise is meant to help you gauge your knowledge of Bible study methods. You are not actually studying the passage at this point, but rather explaining how you *would* study it. Don't be discouraged if you draw a blank. By the end of this workbook you will know which questions to ask and when to ask them—as well as what study tools to use to find answers to your questions.

¹The word of the LORD came to Jonah son of Amittai: ²"Go to the great city of Nineveh and preach against it, because its wickedness has come up before Me."

³But Jonah ran away from the LORD and headed for Tarshish. He went down to Joppa, where he found a ship bound for that port. After paying the fare, he went aboard and sailed for Tarshish to flee from the LORD.

⁴Then the LORD sent a great wind on the sea, and such a violent storm arose that the ship threatened to break up. ⁵All the sailors were afraid and each cried out to his own god. And they threw the cargo into the sea to lighten the ship.

But Jonah had gone below deck, where he lay down and fell into a deep sleep. ⁶The captain went to him and said, "How can you sleep? Get up and call on your god! Maybe he will take notice of us, and we will not perish."

⁷Then the sailors said to each other, "Come, let us cast lots to find out who is responsible for this calamity." They cast lots and the lot fell on Jonah.

⁸So they asked him, "Tell us, who is responsible for making all this trouble for us? What do you do? Where do you come from? What is your country? From what people are you?"

⁹He answered, "I am a Hebrew and I worship the LORD, the God of heaven, who made the sea and the land."

Observe Interpret Apply

¹⁰This terrified them and they asked, "What have you done?" (They knew he was running away from the LORD, because he had already told them so.)

¹¹The sea was getting rougher and rougher. So they asked him, "What should we do to you to make the sea calm down for us?"

¹²"Pick me up and throw me into the sea," he replied, "and it will become calm. I know that it is my fault that this great storm has come upon you."

¹³Instead, the men did their best to row back to land. But they could not, for the sea grew even wilder than before. ¹⁴Then they cried to the LORD, "O LORD, please do not let us die for taking this man's life. Do not hold us accountable for killing an innocent man, for You, O LORD, have done as You pleased." ¹⁵Then they took Jonah and threw him overboard, and the raging sea grew calm. ¹⁶At this the men greatly feared the LORD, and they offered a sacrifice to the LORD and made vows to Him.

¹⁷But the LORD provided a great fish to swallow Jonah, and Jonah was inside the fish three days and three nights.

—Jonah 1:1-17

QUESTION 1: What would you do first to study this passage?

QUESTION 2: Having taken that first step, what would be your next steps in studying this passage? List the steps you would go through to come to a clearer understanding of this passage.

QUESTION 3: If you were studying Ephesians 1 instead of Jonah 1 what (if any) differences might you make in your method of study? List those differences.

QUESTION 4: Survey your current ideas about Bible study. In your opinion, what are the most important principles for sound Bible study? Try to list five principles.

1.

2.

3.

4.

5.

Has this exercise whetted your appetite to know more—more about the Book of Jonah and more about how to study the Bible in general? If these four questions have prompted questions of your own, jot them here. The following chapters will probably address many of your concerns.

My questions about how to study the Bible:

My questions about Jonah 1:

Now let's turn to the first step of inductive Bible study: *observation.*

PART ONE

CHAPTER 3
Step 1: Observation Asks, "What Do I See?"

What is the process of getting to know a new friend? The first step is *observation*. You notice that he stands straight, walks with confidence, that his smile begins first in his eyes, that his voice is both warm and firm. If you are particularly observant, you will also notice that he sometimes drums his fingers restlessly against his leg.

But as you continue to observe your friend, during weeks and years, you constantly find new information. You learn the wide range of expression in his face and voice. You learn his moods, his feelings, his history, his goals, his fears. You learn the character that makes the observable surface a cohesive whole. You learn the reason for his drumming fingers.

We are tempted to assume that observation is quick and casual. But quick and casual is only the first phase of observation. In friendship, observation can take years. In Bible study, initial observation can take hours. But a lifetime of observation will enrich your findings. The story below illustrates how long it took one student to observe a fish. But, as this story will testify, time in observation is time well spent.

Take a few moments to enter the gentle, slow-paced education system of a previous century. Notice the responsibility placed on the student, how and why he learns, what impact that learning has on his emotions, his future techniques of study—even his career. It all began when Professor Agassiz showed a student how to look at what was already familiar and really see: observation.

Observe Interpret Apply

The Student, the Fish, and Agassiz
by the Student

It was more than fifteen years ago that I entered the laboratory of Professor Agassiz, and told him I had enrolled my name in the scientific school as a student of natural history. He asked me a few questions about my object in coming, my antecedents generally, the mode in which I afterwards proposed to use the knowledge I might acquire, and finally, whether I wished to study any special branch. To the latter I replied that while I wished to be well grounded in all departments of zoology, I purposed to devote myself specially to insects.

"When do you wish to begin?" he asked.

"Now," I replied.

This seemed to please him, and with an energetic "Very well," he reached from a shelf a huge jar of specimens in yellow alcohol. "Take this fish," said he, "and look at it; we call it a Haemulon [pronounced Hem-yu' lon]; by and by I will ask what you have seen."

With that he left me, but in a moment returned with explicit instructions as to the care of the object entrusted to me.

"No man is fit to be a naturalist," said he, "who does not know how to take care of specimens."

I was to keep the fish before me in a tin tray, and occasionally moisten the surface with alcohol from the jar, always taking care to replace the stopper tightly. Those were not the days of ground glass stoppers, and elegantly shaped exhibition jars; all the old students will recall the huge, neckless glass bottles with their leaky, wax-besmeared corks half eaten by insects and begrimed with cellar dust. Entomology was a cleaner science than ichthyology, but the example of the professor, who had unhesitatingly plunged to the bottom of the jar to produce the fish, was infectious; and the though this alcohol had "a very ancient and fishlike smell," I really dared not show any aversion within these sacred precincts, and treated the alcohol as though it were pure water. Still I was conscious of a passing feeling of disappointment, for gazing at a fish did not commend itself to an ardent entomologist. My friends at home, too, were annoyed, when they discovered that no amount of eau de Cologne would drown the perfume which haunted me like a shadow.

In ten minutes I had seen all that could be seen in that fish, and started in search of the professor, who had, however, left the museum; and when I returned, after lingering over some of the odd animals stored in the upper apartment, my specimen was dry all over. I dashed the fluid over the fish as if to resuscitate it from a fainting-fit, and looked with anxiety for a return of the normal, sloppy appearance. This little excitement over, nothing was to be done but return to a steadfast gaze at my mute companion. Half an hour passed, an hour, another hour; the fish began to look loathsome. I turned it over and around; looked it in the face—ghastly; from behind, beneath, above, sideways, at a three-quarters' view—just as ghastly. I was in despair; at an early hour I concluded that lunch was necessary; so, with infinite relief, the fish was carefully replaced in the jar, and for an hour I was free.

On my return, I learned that Professor Agassiz had been at the museum, but had gone and would not return for several hours. My fellow students were too busy to be disturbed by continued conversation. Slowly I drew forth that hideous fish, and with a feeling of desperation again looked at it. I might not use a magnifying glass; instruments of all kinds were interdicted. My

Step 1: Observation Asks, "What Do I See?"

two hands, my two eyes, and the fish; it seemed a most limited field. I pushed my finger down its throat to feel how sharp its teeth were. I begin to count the scales in the different rows until I was convinced that that was nonsense. At last a happy thought struck me—I would draw the fish; and now with surprise I began to discover new features in the creature. Just then the professor returned.

"That is right," said he; "a pencil is one of the best of eyes. I am glad to notice, too, that you keep your specimen wet and your bottle corked."

With these encouraging words he added, "Well, what is it like?"

He listened attentively to my brief rehearsal of the structure of parts whose names were still unknown to me: the fringed gill-arches and movable operculum; the pores of the head, fleshy lips, and lidless eyes; the lateral line, the spinous fin, and forked tail; the compressed and arched body. When I had finished, he waited as if expecting more, and then with an air of disappointment, "You have not looked very carefully; why," he continued, more earnestly, "you haven't seen one of the most conspicuous features of the animal, which is as plainly before your eyes as the fish itself; look again, look again!" and he left me to my misery.

I was piqued; I was mortified. Still more of that wretched fish! But now I set myself to my task with a will, and discovered one new thing after another, until I saw how just the professor's criticism had been. The afternoon passed quickly, and when, towards its close, the professor inquired, "Do you see it yet?"

"No," I replied, "I am certain I do not, but I see how little I saw before."

"That is next best," he said earnestly, "but I won't hear you now; put away your fish and go home; perhaps you will be ready with a better answer in the morning. I will examine you before you look at the fish."

This was disconcerting; not only must I think of my fish all night, studying, without the object before me, what this unknown but most visible feature might be; but also, without reviewing my new discoveries, I must give an exact account of them the next day. I had a bad memory; so I walked home by Charles River in a distracted state, with my two perplexities.

The cordial greeting from the professor the next morning was reassuring; here was a man who seemed to be quite as anxious as I that I should see for myself what he saw.

"Do you perhaps mean," I asked, "that the fish has symmetrical sides with paired organs?"

His thoroughly pleased, "Of course, of course!" repaid the wakeful hours of the previous night. After he had discoursed most happily and enthusiastically—as he always did—upon the importance of this point, I ventured to ask what I should do next.

"Oh, look at your fish!" he said, and left me again to my own devices. In a little more than an hour he returned and heard my new catalogue.

"That is good, that is good!" he repeated, "but that is not all; go on." And so, for three long days, he placed that fish before my eyes, forbidding me to look at anything else, or to use any artificial aid. "Look, look, look," was his repeated injunction.

This was the best entomological lesson I ever had—a lesson whose influence has extended to the details of every subsequent study; a legacy the professor has left to me, as he has left it to many others, of inestimable value, which we could not buy, with which we cannot part.

A year afterwards, some of us were amusing ourselves with chalking outlandish beasts upon the museum blackboard. We drew prancing star-fishes; frogs in mortal combat; hydra-headed worms; stately crawfishes, standing on their tails, bearing aloft umbrellas; and grotesque fishes, with gaping mouths and staring eyes. The professor came in shortly after, and was as amused as any, at our experiments. He looked at the fishes.

"Haemulons, every one of them," he said; "Mr. _____ drew them."

True; and to this day, if I attempt a fish, I can draw nothing but Haemulons.

The fourth day, a second fish of the same group was placed beside the first, and I was bidden to point out the resemblances and differences between the two; another and another followed, until the entire family lay before me, and a whole legion of jars covered the table and surrounding shelves; the odor had become a pleasant perfume; and even now, the sight of an old, six-inch, worm-eaten cork brings fragrant memories!

The whole group of Haemulons was thus brought in review; and, whether engaged upon the dissection of the internal organs, the preparation and examination of the bony framework, or the description of the various parts, Agassiz's training in the method of observing facts and their orderly arrangement was ever accompanied by the urgent exhortation not to be content with them.

"Facts are stupid things," he would say, "until brought into connection with some general law."

At the end of eight months, it was almost with reluctance that I left these friends and turned to insects; but what I had gained by this outside experience has been of greater value than years of later investigation in my favorite groups.[1]

All of us probably have a story similar to the student's—an interest in a discipline or hobby tested by the reality of hard work. At first we couldn't see any immediate pay-off for all our efforts, but gradually we came to appreciate the value of making that initial investment of time and energy. As a result, our interest in the subject not only grew, it deepened. Just like the student in the fish story.

If you haven't already experienced this kind of frustration-turned-reward in studying the Bible, don't worry. You will! Like everything of value in life, studying Scripture is hard work. But the rewards make it all worth it. In this introduction to the first step of inductive Bible study, we will be learning how to lay a solid foundation by observing the facts; this is our initial investment toward knowing and loving God more deeply. The benefit of these observations may not be obvious right away, but stick with it. The hard work *will* bear fruit.

Suppose you set aside an hour this evening to study the Bible. Perhaps when you looked at Jonah 1 in the previous chapter you were intrigued by God's pursuit of Jonah—going so far as to send a giant fish to swallow him! You decide you'd like to know more about this story. So, with your Bible open to the Book of Jonah, you ask yourself, "How do I get started?"

We begin by observing the facts. Taking a close look at what is actually in the text, observation answers the question, "What do I see?" The key to sound Bible study is knowing what to look for, and that is what the next few chapters will address. Learning

Step 1: Observation Asks, "What Do I See?"

the appropriate questions to ask, in the proper sequence, yields the most from our study, whether it is one hour at night or twenty-five hours for a sermon series.

Now you will have an opportunity to study Jonah 1 in more depth. Your assignment here is to observe this passage as carefully as you can.

YOUR TURN

Take fifteen minutes and write down all the significant things you see in Jonah 1. Summarize in your own words the main points and content. Without looking ahead at the box on page 27, try to come up with a list of fifteen or twenty observations (*who, what, where,* and *when*). Feel free to mark up the text with circles, arrows, underlines—whatever is helpful for you to see the facts and relationships in the passage. Note: There is not a list of right and wrong answers for this exercise. The main point is for you to try to see all that is in the passage.

¹The word of the Lord *came to Jonah son of Amittai:* ²*"Go to the great city of Nineveh and preach against it, because its wickedness has come up before Me."*

³But Jonah ran away from the Lord *and headed for Tarshish. He went down to Joppa, where he found a ship bound for that port. After paying the fare, he went aboard and sailed for Tarshish to flee from the* Lord.

⁴Then the Lord *sent a great wind on the sea, and such a violent storm arose that the ship threatened to break up.* ⁵*All the sailors were afraid and each cried out to his own god. And they threw the cargo into the sea to lighten the ship.*

But Jonah had gone below deck, where he lay down and fell into a deep sleep. ⁶*The captain went to him and said, "How can you sleep? Get up and call on your god! Maybe he will take notice of us, and we will not perish."*

⁷Then the sailors said to each other, "Come, let us cast lots to find out who is responsible for this calamity." They cast lots and the lot fell on Jonah.

⁸So they asked him, "Tell us, who is responsible for making all this trouble for us? What do you do? Where do you come from? What is your country? From what people are you?"

⁹He answered, "I am a Hebrew and I worship the Lord, *the God of heaven, who made the sea and the land."*

¹⁰This terrified them and they asked, "What have you done?" (They knew he was running away from the Lord, *because he had already told them so.)*

¹¹The sea was getting rougher and rougher. So they asked him, "What should we do to you to make the sea calm down for us?"

¹²"Pick me up and throw me into the sea," he replied, "and it will become calm. I know that it is my fault that this great storm has come upon you."

¹³Instead, the men did their best to row back to land. But they could not, for the sea grew even wilder than before. ¹⁴*Then they cried to the* LORD, *"O* LORD, *please do not let us die for taking this man's life. Do not hold us accountable for killing an innocent man, for You, O* LORD, *have done as You pleased."* ¹⁵*Then they took Jonah and threw him overboard, and the raging sea grew calm.* ¹⁶*At this the men greatly feared the* LORD, *and they offered a sacrifice to the* LORD *and made vows to Him.*

¹⁷*But the* LORD *provided a great fish to swallow Jonah, and Jonah was inside the fish three days and three nights.*

—Jonah 1:1-17

Observations on Jonah 1

1.

2.

3.

4.

5.

6.

7.

8.

9.

10.

11.

12.

13.

Step 1: Observation Asks, "What Do I See?"

14.

15.

16.

17.

18.

19.

20.

21.

22.

23.

24.

25.

26.

27.

28.

29.

30.

If you were able to make fifteen or more observations that's great, but if not don't worry. You will find more opportunities to practice observing the details of a passage in the coming chapters. On page 27 is a list of initial observations with which to compare your answers. They are only a few of the many observations one might make on the passage.

Observation in Three Steps

The process of observation can be divided into three stages of study, moving from the general to the specific. First, we look at the *whole,* then divide that up into its *parts,* and finally scrutinize the *details.*

The process of starting with the whole and working toward the details is like a miner who searches for precious gems. He begins by asking: "Where is the best mountain to dig for precious gems?" He could use an airplane or even satellite photos to get the big picture of the region's topography (the *whole*). A careful overview of the whole section of terrain leads him to a specific range of mountains (the *parts*) that promises him the greatest success. Then he goes deep into the mountain and begins to pick away at specific veins of mineral-rich earth (the *details*). If the miner had begun digging in a randomly chosen hole without first getting a broad overview, his efforts would have been counterproductive. The same holds true for effective Bible study.

Intuition tells us to look at the whole of something before examining it in detail. Whether we are planning to buy a painting in an art gallery or a car from a used car lot, we first look at the object as a whole. If the car looks good from a distance (the paint job looks good, or there are no dents in the frame), we may decide to take a closer look and do a few observation tests of our own (kick the tires, look under the hood). In a final inspection of the details, we may even take the car to a mechanic for a more in-depth analysis. The same process should happen in Bible study—beginning with a general overview we work toward the specific issues. It's difficult (and sometimes impossible) to correctly understand and appreciate the details of a text without first having a grasp of the whole picture.

When it comes to studying Scripture, all that preliminary investigation can seem unnecessary—but it is essential. Bible study requires hard work, but the rewards are worth it. When I find that jewel of truth for myself it is much more thrilling than if someone had handed it to me on a velvet pillow. As you work through these next few chapters you'll see what I mean.

Step 1: Observation Asks, "What Do I See?"

Initial Observations on Jonah 1

1. God told Jonah to go to Nineveh and preach (vv. 1-2).
2. Nineveh was an evil place (v. 2).
3. Jonah disobeyed God and went to Tarshish (v. 3).
4. Jonah took a boat to Tarshish (v. 3).
5. God caused a fierce storm to blow against the ship (v. 4).
6. The people on board feared for their lives (v. 5).
7. In the midst of the storm Jonah went to sleep below deck (v. 5).
8. The captain believed Jonah's "god" could save them (v. 6).
9. The crew cast lots to see who was to blame for the storm (v. 7).
10. The lot fell on Jonah (v. 7).
11. Jonah declared God to be the Maker of the sea and land (v. 9).
12. Jonah said to throw him overboard to calm the storm (v. 12).
13. The crew tried to row ashore instead of sacrificing Jonah (v. 13).
14. The storm intensified (v. 13).
15. The crew asked God's forgiveness for sacrificing Jonah (v. 14).
16. The sea became calm after Jonah was thrown into it (v. 15).
17. The crew revered God because He calmed the sea (v. 16).
18. God sent a huge fish to swallow Jonah (v. 17).
19. Jonah lived inside the fish for three days and nights (v. 17).

CHAPTER 4
Looking at the Whole

The first essential for observing the whole of a passage or book of the Bible is to read it. Sounds simple, right? It is simple—to understand, that is, but it can be hard to make time to do.

One of the most common reasons many Christians are not strengthened by the Bible's teaching is that they spend too little time simply reading it for themselves. The result? Spiritual malnutrition. One of the primary ways to develop our relationship with Christ is to spend time in the pages of God's revealed truth.

In doing observation, we must spend blocks of time in quiet, concentrated reading. As basic as this may sound, there is just no substitute for reading and rereading Scripture. There is a place for consulting books about the Bible, but we'll discuss this later. In this initial phase of inductive study, the Bible is our source of information. So, how should we read Scripture?

1. Read the Passage with Care.
Read repeatedly. Take time to read your text several times (even out loud) to become familiar with its general message. It is amazing how an overall grasp of the contents lays the groundwork for fruitful study.

Read thoughtfully. Focus your attention on the text. Our minds can wander when we read the Bible or when we pray. Sometimes it seems that the best way to remember what we

Looking at the Whole

forgot to do is to sit down to read the Bible. Instantly, the things we left undone come to mind and tempt us to go do them. Many of the principles discussed in this workbook will help you concentrate when reading Scripture. One practical suggestion is to write down your thoughts as you read and study. You may even want to keep a journal of what you learn. And for those distracting thoughts, keep a notepad nearby to write down any jobs you've left undone around the home or office. You won't forget them, but you also won't feel compelled to go do them right away either.

Read patiently. Take time to fellowship with God. As busy as our lives are, we need to find time for unhurried reading. "Free time" is so hard to find for most of us that it is necessary to schedule it as a regular part of our day.

Don't underestimate the value of simply reading the Bible. It is the essential foundation for solid observation, interpretation, and application.

2. Record Your Initial Impressions.
After reading the text, jot down your overall impression of the text. Then note more specific impressions. (This is similar to what you did with the Jonah 1 passage.) At this point you are creating a framework for understanding the contents of the passage.

What happens when you meet a person for the first time? Without even being conscious of it, don't you form an initial impression of the person—making certain observations about him or her? Although you don't yet have a complete picture of the person, *observation* is how you begin to understand that person. That is the same reason why we begin our study of a text by making note of our first impressions or observations—to lay a foundation upon which to build understanding.

YOUR TURN

Using Philippians 2:1-11, practice the first two steps in *observing the whole.*

1. Read the passage with care. Read through Philippians 2:1-11 several times in one sitting. (Approximate time: 10 minutes)

Observe Interpret Apply

2. Record you initial impressions. Reflecting on what you have read, record your general impression of the text. Then write twelve to fifteen more specific impressions of this passage. (Approximate time: 15 minutes)

3. Record the Major Facts. Now that you have read the passage and written down your initial impressions, it's time to go back and hunt for more information. Observing the whole involves discovering the facts in a passage. These facts can be gathered by answering key questions; observation is simply knowing what questions to ask. Four words can help us to uncover facts: *who, what, where,* and *when.*

Looking at the Whole

Who? Who is speaking and who are the listeners? Who are the characters involved, and what can we learn about them? Identify all the principle characters in the passage.

What? What is happening? Is the passage about events or ideas? What is the main subject, and what are the key words? What is the tone of the passage; does it reflect joy, sorrow, victory, defeat? What took place before or after the events described in this passage that might help you to understand it?

Where? Describe the location of the action. Where is the author at the time he is writing and where are the recipients? Are there important geographical locations that need to be identified on a map in order to understand the setting of the text?

When? When are these events taking place? Is the timing significant? At what point in the history of Israel or the church is this event occurring? Is the timing important in the life of the author or the recipients?

You may be wondering about the question *why*. That question is reserved for the next step of inductive Bible study, *interpretation*. Chapters 7 and 8 provide several opportunities to practice the *why* of Bible study which gets at the meaning behind the facts observed.

In the step of observing the whole of a passage, we are searching for its general structure. Looking first at a passage or book as a whole can give us fresh understanding of it—perhaps ideas we never heard in a sermon or Sunday School class.

YOUR TURN

This exercise is an extension of the other two you completed earlier in the chapter. Still using Philippians 2:1-11, practice the third step in *observing the whole*.

3. Record the major facts. With your Bible open before you, begin answering the four key questions of who, what, where, and when. Make a list of observations based on these questions, trying to come up with at least ten for each category. (Approximate time: 30 minutes)

Observe Interpret Apply

Who?

What?

Where?

When?

CHAPTER 5
Looking at the Parts

Every portion of Scripture, whether it deals with ideas or events, has organization. This organization can be broken down into divisions, or parts, which reveal the way the author arranged his thoughts or the events described. Having familiarized yourself with the Philippians passage as a whole, it's time to look at how Paul structured his thoughts. The term *structure* here means the relationship of ideas or actions to one another within the passage or book being studied.

Understanding the principles of structure is an essential part of determining the logic of a passage. Using the principles listed on the following page will help reveal the relationships between ideas and events. These principles are discussed in greater detail using examples from Scripture in Appendix C. You may want to refer to it for illustrations of each principle.

To illustrate how to determine the structure of a passage, read Galatians 5:16-26, looking for how Paul structures his concepts in these verses. One way that Paul develops his ideas about living in the Spirit is through the use of *contrast*. Write out several examples.

Contrast in Galatians 5:16-26

Observe Interpret Apply

Contrast in Galatians 5:16-26, continued

THE PRINCIPLES OF STRUCTURE

COMPARISON: associating things which are alike.

CONTRAST: associating things which are opposite.

REPETITION: reiterating the same or similar terms, phrases, clauses, or concepts.

CAUSE TO EFFECT: stating a cause and then its effect(s).

EFFECT TO CAUSE: stating or describing an effect and then its cause.

EXPLANATION: introducing an idea which is then expanded or clarified.

ILLUSTRATION: introducing an idea, followed by an example of it.

CLIMAX: arranging the text so that it progresses from the lesser to the greater (i.e., the story or discourse builds to a climax).

PIVOT: arranging the subject matter so that there are specific points at which the story changes direction; they act like hinges in the text.

INTERCHANGE: altering or exchanging certain elements in the text; moving back and forth between several ideas.

PREPARATION: including background material or the setting for events or ideas to prepare the reader to understand what follows.

SUMMARY: briefly restating the main ideas presented.

QUESTION POSED: structuring the text around questions the author raises.

QUESTION ANSWERED: structuring the text around answers the author gives to a question, either explicitly stated or merely implied.

How do we find these principles in a passage? An outline, diagram, or chart can bring the structure of a passage into focus. One such device for seeing the relationships between the words or ideas expressed in a text is the *structural outline*—the term *structure* referring to the way things are put together. A structural outline shows the logic in a passage by writing out the phrases of the verses in short lines. The outline of Romans

8:35-39 below illustrates this technique. Notice how Paul uses the *question posed* principle (in boldface type) in this passage.

STRUCTURAL OUTLINE
Romans 8:35, 38-39

Who shall separate us from the love of Christ?   (Question Posed)

Shall trouble
    or hardship
    or persecution
    or famine   (Repetition)
    or nakedness
    or danger
    or sword? . . .

For I am convinced that
    neither death
    nor life,
    neither angels
    nor demons,
    neither the present   (Contrast)
    nor the future,
    nor any powers,
    neither height
    nor depth,

nor anything else in all creation,   (Climax)

will be able to separate us from the love of God that is in Christ Jesus our Lord.

For another example, look at the following structural outline developed for Galatians 5:16-26. Notice how it combines the two techniques described in this chapter—finding the *principles of structure* by using a *structural outline*.

THE VERTICAL CHART
The Structural Outline & Principles of Structure
Galatians 5:16-26

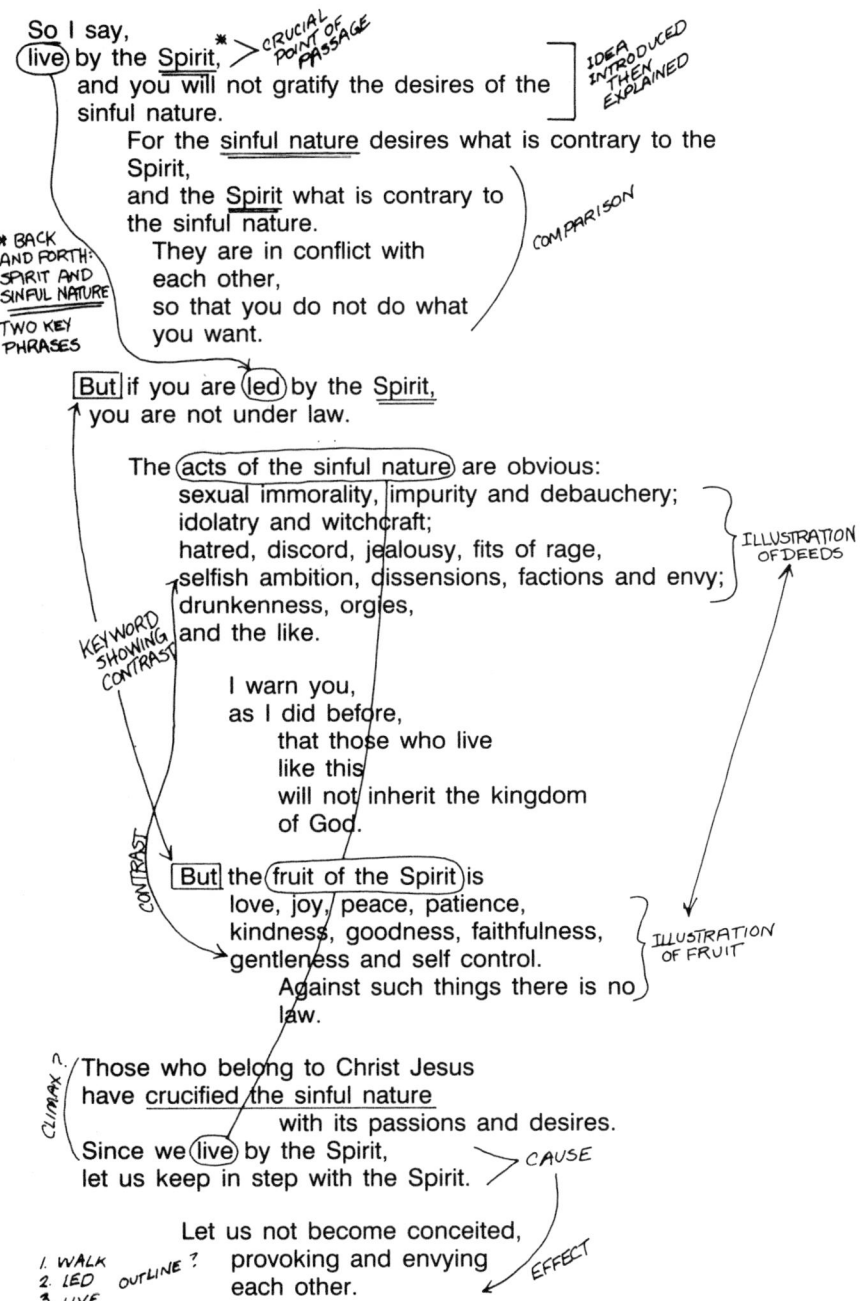

Observe Interpret Apply

When I study a passage or book of Scripture, this exercise of charting the text is probably the most important step for me as I try to determine what the author had in mind. As I said at the beginning, my passion is to make Bible study simpler, not more overwhelming. Although making a chart may seem a little intimidating if you've never done it, your study will actually be made easier because you will be able to *see* the relationships between words and ideas. Many of us are visual learners; if we can see it we can understand it. This exercise allows you to visualize how the author organized his thoughts.

The vertical chart on page 37 was produced by first writing out the contents of Galatians 5:15-26 in a structural way and then identifying the structural relationships that became obvious. To do this, read down the list of principles of structure on page 35 and see if any of them occur in your passage. (Using colored pens helps distinguish different ideas you find.) Once you've completed a vertical chart for a passage, it's relatively simple to produce an outline of the passage structure like the example below.

YOUR TURN

After you have studied the structural outline and principles of structure for Galatians 5:16-26, try to find the structure of Philippians 2:1-11. Write out the verses in a structural outline in the space provided. Then, mark the principles of structure on your outline with lines, circles, and squares, jotting down notes to yourself. Finally, write a brief outline of the passage like the one below for Galatians. (Approximate time: 90 minutes)

Outline of Galatians 5:16-26

1. *Exhortation:* live by the Spirit (v. 16)

2. *Negative example:* acts of the sinful nature (vv. 17-21)

3. *Positive example:* fruit of the Spirit (vv. 22-23)

4. *Conclusion:* Christians should walk by the Spirit because they have crucified the sinful nature (vv. 24-26)

Looking at the Parts

VERTICAL CHART
The Structural Outline and Principles of Structure
Philippians 2:1-11

BRIEF OUTLINE OF PHILIPPIANS 2:1-11

CHAPTER 6
Looking at the Details

On April 10, 1940, *The New York Times* ran the following advertisement for Mortimer Adler's *How to Read a Book*. At the top was a picture of a puzzled youth reading his first love letter.

How to Read a Love Letter

This young man has just received his first love letter. He may have already read it three or four times, but he is just beginning. To read it as accurately as he would like, would require several dictionaries and a good deal of close work with a few experts on etymology and philology.

However, he will do all right without them.

He will ponder over the exact shade of meaning of every word, every comma. She has headed the letter "Dear John." What, he asks himself, is the exact significance of those words? Did she refrain from saying "Dearest" because she was bashful? Would "My Dear" have sounded too formal?

Jeepers, maybe she would have said "Dear So-and-So" to anybody!

A worried frown will now appear on his face. But it disappears as soon as he really gets to thinking about the first sentence. She certainly wouldn't have written that to anybody!

And so he works his way through the letter, one moment perched blissfully on a cloud, the next moment huddled miserably behind an eight-ball. It has started a hundred questions in his mind. He could quote it by heart. In fact, he will—to himself—for weeks to come.*

---

*COPYRIGHT © 1940 by Simon & Schuster, Inc. Reprinted by permission of Pocket Books, a division of Simon & Schuster, Inc.

Observe Interpret Apply

We read and reread the things that we know affect us personally—like love letters. Every detail, every nuance is important to us. The same is true of reading Scripture; the more we experience the truths of the Bible in our own lives, the more we want to pore over its contents to try to understand every detail. We have discussed how to look at the whole of a passage, then at its various *parts*. In this chapter we will discuss how to observe the *details* of a Bible passage or book.

By now, you have probably run across a number of interesting items in your study that you would like to research further. Perhaps you were struck by a key word or a certain character. In this phase of observation you will closely examine these details. Even though you will continue to focus on the main text, at this stage you will also examine the context (within the same book) for clues.

The Questions of Observation
During this final phase of observation, you will isolate those details that stand out in the passage—details that raise questions or need to be more fully explained. The following list summarizes the questions related to the details of a passage. Note that this list is an expansion of the information covered in chapter 4.

Who? (the characters)	Where? (the geography and location)
☐ The writer ☐ The recipients ☐ The characters involved in the action ☐ The characters indirectly involved in the action ☐ Special people addressed in the passage	☐ Places mentioned ☐ Buildings ☐ Cities ☐ Nations ☐ Landmarks

What? (the key truths or events)	When? (the time factors)
☐ Key ideas ☐ Theological terms ☐ Key events ☐ Important words (verb tense, commands) ☐ Figures of speech ☐ Atmosphere	☐ Date of author's writing ☐ Duration of the action ☐ At what point in the life of Israel ☐ At what point in the life of the church ☐ Past, present, or future

The following chart will give you an idea of how to record your study of the details. Notice the details in Colossians 1:24-29 and the questions raised by some of those details.

A STUDY OF THE DETAILS
Colossians 1:24-29

Interesting Details	Questions	Possible Answers
Who? (the characters)		
Paul and Timothy are writing (1:1)	Where are they when writing?	
The church at Colossae is the one Paul is suffering for (1:2, 24)	What is causing his suffering?	
The church at Colossae is a Gentile church (1:27)	Did Paul help start this church?	
The church seems to be a central "character" here Paul suffers for the church Paul works for the church The mystery is the church	How often is *church* mentioned in the book?	
The letter is meant not only for the church at Colossae, but also the church at Laodicea (4:16)		
What? (key truths or events)		
The church is a key idea; seems to be speaking of the universal church—Christ's body (1:24)		
The *mystery* is a key idea (1:26-27) Paul's message is this mystery (1:25-26)	Look up concept of *mystery* in the N.T.	
Key concept: Christ in you; this is the mystery (1:27)	What does this mean?	
Other key words: body (1:24) servant (1:25) admonishing (1:28) perfect in Christ (1:28)		
Paul is working—laboring and striving—in spite of being in jail (1:29)		
Where? (geography and location)		
Paul is in prison (4:3)	Is Timothy also? Are they in Rome? Look up Colossae on a Bible map.	
When? (time factors)		
The church at Colossae seems fully developed, with a rich past (1:3-9)		
Paul is in prison, nearing the final days of his work (4:3)		
Past ages did not know about the mystery (1:26)	What is he referring to by past *ages and generations*?	
Paul expresses his anticipation for the future (1:28)		

Observe Interpret Apply

Notice that not every detail on the left-hand side of the chart has a corresponding question. Many of the items you will note will be simple observations of what you see in the passage. Some details you observe will require answers. As was said earlier, for now don't be concerned to answer all of these questions, simply locate and isolate those you want to know more about.

Don't Let Details Overwhelm You
Many of the specifics of a passage could themselves be the subject of a future topical Bible study. The more time you can give to your study, the more rich it will be, but remember to leave adequate time for interpretation and application. If you cannot take time to answer all of the questions raised by details in the text, make a note of items you would like to study in the future. In this type of study try to discern the main details and clarify them.

The following exercise for observing details completes your observation of Philippians 2:1-11.

YOUR TURN

Here you will investigate some of the interesting details of Philippians 2:1-11. Using the example of Colossians 1:24-29 and the list of details to look for on page 42, choose a dozen or so items that interest you most and record them on the pages that follow.

A STUDY OF THE DETAILS
Philippians 2:1-11

Interesting Details	Questions	Possible Answers

Who? (the characters)

Looking at the Details

What? (key truths or events)

Where? (geography and location)

When? (time factors)

You have now completed the first step in learning how to study the Bible: *observation*. The next phase of inductive Bible study, *interpretation*, will explore how to discover the meaning of the facts in a passage of Scripture.

CHAPTER 7

Step 2: Interpretation Asks, "What Does It Mean?"

I recently read the tragic story of a group of people who died in a fire at a banquet hall because of an ironic twist of information. When the fire broke out panic ensued. Everyone naturally fled to doorways marked exit. They did not know that one major doorway of the large room was locked and barricaded from the outside. When the fire was finally out, police found dozens of people huddled against the locked door—they all died because of a misinterpretation. They assumed (understandably) that an exit sign meant that they could get out. That assumption took their lives.

Without having all the facts, and then bringing them together, we can misinterpret what is actually going on in a situation. By now you've spent several hours observing the facts in Philippians 2:1-11. But these facts, if they are going to be useful, need to be brought into relationship with one another. *Interpretation* is the step where you pull all the facts together into a coherent explanation of their meaning. This is also where you will investigate any puzzling details in the passage. Although the following systematic approach to interpreting facts may be new to you, in reality you do it all the time—without even thinking about it. In this chapter we hope to take those unconscious skills and hone them.

To illustrate the process of interpretation, let's again use the example of buying a car. You have studied the car carefully, kicked the tires, poked under the hood, taken it for a drive, and even had a mechanic look it over. You've gathered all the facts. Finally, you conclude that it is a bad investment because the facts indicate the car is a lemon. That's interpretation—determining the meaning once all the facts are in. The more time you spend

Step 2: Interpretation Asks, "What Does It Mean?"

gathering information, the more accurate your interpretation will be; interpretation is built on thorough observation.

Careful observation, however, does not *guarantee* accurate interpretation. Sometimes people can make careful observations and completely misinterpret the facts. The following story by a ten-year-old who studied a cow illustrates this point.

> The cow is a mammal. It has six sides—right, left, an upper, and below. At the back it has a tail on which hangs a brush. With this it sends the flies away so that they do not fall into the milk. The head is for the purpose of growing horns and so that the mouth can be somewhere. The horns are to butt with, and the mouth is to moo with. Under the cow hangs the milk. It is arranged for milking. When people milk, the milk comes and there is never an end to the supply. How the cow does this I have not yet realized, but it makes more and more. . . . The man cow is called an ox. It is not a mammal. The cow does not eat much, but what it eats it eats twice, so that it gets enough.
> When it is hungry it moos, and when it says nothing it is because its inside is all full up with grass.[1]

Interpretation brings meaning to the facts. The child was full of observations but he brought faulty meaning to the facts he observed. This chapter and the next will discuss how to guard against drawing the wrong conclusions from a text. A word of caution however: *No method of interpretation is "foolproof."*

Let's consider how interpretation relates to the Bible by using the Philippians 2:1-11 passage from chapter 6. What does the passage mean? Are there several messages? Do you need to discover more about the meaning of significant words in the text? This is the time to ask: What was the author trying to say?

Interpretation: Discovering the Author's Intention

Whether we are focusing on a work of art, a poem, a sermon, or a passage of Scripture, there is a logical demand for meaning; there is a need to answer the question, "What is the author/artist trying to say?" In the case of Scripture, the ultimate question is, "What was God saying through the biblical writers?" (The question of what a text means for us today is a separate question and is reserved for the last stage: *application*.)

Have you ever wished you could understand spiritual truths the way the Apostle Paul did? What was he really thinking when he said in Philippians 2:3, "Do nothing out of selfish ambition or vain conceit"? Did he mean that all ambition is wrong? Why is selfish ambition and vain conceit an opposite to being united with Christ? What are we saying about ourselves and other believers if we refuse to indulge in selfish ambition and vain conceit? *Interpretation* answers questions like these. It is the work of trying to get inside the author's head (and heart) to determine what he intended his readers to understand.

Identifying with the author involves trying to reconstruct the historical context in which he wrote. An effective Bible teacher tries to reconstruct the meaning of the text as if he or she were actually the writer. It is something like the great conductor Toscanini bringing to life the music of Beethoven.

> While rehearsing Beethoven's "Ninth Symphony," the musicians responded with a particular sensitivity to Toscanini's every wish and desire. What resulted was a performance that moved the men of the orchestra to a spontaneous ovation. They rose to their feet and cheered the little man who had just given them such a new and wonderful insight into the music. Desperately, Toscanini tried to stop them, waving his arms wildly, shouting to them. Finally when the ovation subsided, he said in a broken voice: "It isn't me, men—it's Beethoven."[2]

When interpreting Scripture, our objective is the same as Toscanini's. It isn't *our* meaning but the writer's original intent that we are after—and ultimately that of God Himself, communicating His truth through the writer. I cannot stress this point enough. We try to discover God's intent by asking questions of interpretation—and then answering them.

Principles of Interpretation
Interpreting the Bible is not always easy. The Westminster Confession reads: "All things in Scripture are not alike plain in themselves, nor alike clear unto all." Charles Spurgeon said that when he faced Scriptures he could not understand he simply had to kneel down and worship God. But even if we cannot understand all that mystifies us in Scripture, we can relax in the assurance that the central messages of the Bible are clear for all. As Irving Jensen says, "Everything essential to salvation and Christian living is clearly revealed in Scripture."[3]

The process of interpretation is known by the technical term *hermeneutics*. The word comes from the Greek *hermeneuo,* meaning "to interpret or explain," as in Luke 24:27: "And beginning with Moses and all the Prophets, he [Jesus] explained to them what was said in all the Scriptures concerning himself." The word is also derived from the name of the Greek mythological god Hermes, the messenger of the gods. He interpreted the will of the gods to the people.

Volumes have been written on the subject of interpretation. The following four principles are an overview of a process for sound interpretation. Keep these principles in mind whenever you ask questions of interpretation. Consider committing them to memory.

1. Let Scripture interpret Scripture. This is the first tenet of the Reformation, known in Latin as *Sacra Scriptura sui interpres,* "Sacred Scripture is its own interpreter." It means that the Bible does not contradict itself; it is internally consistent in its teaching. When we are deriving the meaning of a passage or book of Scripture, our conclusions must be

Step 2: Interpretation Asks, "What Does It Mean?"

compatible with the other teachings of the Bible. The Bible has one author, God, and His message is coherent and harmonious.

2. Interpret the Bible literally. In general, the most accurate meaning of a text is the most obvious one. The Bible simply means what it says. This principle requires some qualification, however, in order to be useful. The Bible is literature, and therefore, its words should first be understood in their historic context, having the intended meaning in the usage of that day. But there is a great deal of figurative language in the Bible, and these texts must be understood according to special rules of interpretation not generally applied to the rest of Scripture. (These rules are discussed in Part Two.)

3. Interpret the Bible grammatically. The words of Scripture are to be interpreted in their natural sense, according to ordinary rules of grammar. This means that generally:

- ☐ a word has only one meaning when used in a sentence (again, exceptions to this rule are discussed in Part Two)
- ☐ a word's meaning is tied to the sentence by rules of grammar
- ☐ the meaning of a word must be derived from its context

For example, the word *run* can have several, completely different meanings, depending on its context in a sentence. A run can refer to a score in baseball, or a tear in a woman's stockings, or a streak of good luck—only the rest of the sentence can help us decide which meaning is intended by the speaker.

4. Interpret the Bible in its historical setting. The Bible is the story of God working in human history, a record of events that actually happened. For this reason we must study Scripture in light of the historical times in which it was written. Many things have changed since Bible times, so the more we learn of the author's setting, lifestyle, and culture, the more accurate our interpretation (and therefore our application) will be.

The Questions of Interpretation

In chapter 6 you practiced observing the details by asking four questions: *who, what, where,* and *when,* leaving questions of *why* unanswered for the time being. In this chapter we will discuss the steps of interpretation and have a chance to practice a few of them. In chapter 8 you will be asked to go back and answer (or refine your answers to) the questions you came up with when you gathered information on Philippians 2:1-11.

The goal is to discover what the author meant by those items in question. At the interpretive stage, you will go beyond collecting the facts expressed in the biblical text. Even though you ask many of the same questions that you asked at the observation stage, you will now be asking yourself: *What additional research* do I need to do in order to find out more about the meaning and significance of:

Who? (the characters)
- ☐ The writer
- ☐ The recipients
- ☐ The characters involved in the action
- ☐ The characters indirectly involved in the action
- ☐ Special people addressed in the passage

What? (the key truths or events)
- ☐ Key ideas
- ☐ Theological terms
- ☐ Key events
- ☐ Important words (verb tense, commands)
- ☐ Figures of speech
- ☐ Atmosphere

Where? (the geography and location)
- ☐ Places mentioned
- ☐ Buildings
- ☐ Cities
- ☐ Nations
- ☐ Landmarks

When? (the time factors)
- ☐ Date of author's writing
- ☐ Duration of the action
- ☐ At what point in the life of Israel
- ☐ At what point in the life of the church
- ☐ Past, present, or future

There is one more question that we want to answer at the interpretation stage of Bible study. This question summarizes your interpretation of the *purpose* of the passage or book being studied, and therefore comes last.

Why? (the purpose of the passage or book)
- ☐ The readers' need
- ☐ The writer's message

This question of purpose is two-sided. On the one hand, there is the need that caused the revelation to be given; on the other the author's message which addressed that need. First, what is the readers' need? What central concern do you find the writer addressing in the passage or book? Why was it necessary for the author to write? This *need* question could also be called the "problem" that the message was meant to "solve." Not all

Step 2: Interpretation Asks, "What Does It Mean?"

Scripture addresses problems (Ephesians, for example does not), but typically there was something happening in the lives of the readers that prompted the author to write. Suppose your son called to tell you about marriage problems he was having. You'd want to give him sound advice. Perhaps you would write your advice in a letter, so that he could reflect on your thoughts. The *need* is the marital problems; the *message* is your advice.

▶ *The Reader's Need:* The reason why the author wrote the passage or book.

▶ *The Writer's Message:* The answers or solutions the writer gave to address the need.

Finding these two elements in a passage or book is hard work, and requires diligent thinking. You must draw conclusions based on all you have previously studied.

YOUR TURN

Let's practice this last question of interpretation. Reread Philippians 2:1-11. What do you think is the Philippians' need and what is Paul's message that addresses their need?

▶ The Philippians' need:

▶ Paul's message:

The Answers for Interpretation
We've discussed the questions to ask when interpreting the facts of a passage: *who, what, where, when,* and *why*. Now we will look at how to go about answering those questions. The 5 C's of interpretation are: *content, context, comparison, consultation,* and *conclusion*.

1. State an initial proposal based on the content. What do you think is the answer to your question? We all come to the Bible with preconceived ideas about what the text means — write that idea down, and test your hypothesis as you work through the other stages of interpretation. Remember, your interpretation should come from the passage you are studying, not from referring to someone else's idea of what the passage means.

Observe Interpret Apply

2. Search the context. The teaching of a passage of Scripture must be viewed within the setting of the book in which it is located. How do the surrounding verses (the paragraphs before and after, the chapter before and after, the whole book) help you understand it? Knowing the purpose and development of the book as a whole will automatically narrow your thinking about any individual part. This is one way of letting Scripture interpret itself.

3. Seek biblical comparisons. The Bible, though it contains many different parts, speaks with one unified voice. Sound interpretation always takes into account the whole teaching of Scripture. Use the cross-references found in the margins of many Bibles to compare the verses you are studying with related passages found elsewhere in the Bible. Taking into account the context of each new reference look up those verses and see what they say about the subject you are examining. Then look at several different translations of your passage to get a fuller range of meaning for certain words or concepts. Also, use a concordance to look up similar teachings or topics mentioned in other places in Scripture. (See Appendix A for the definition and uses of a concordance, as well as other Bible study aids.)

4. Consult the secondary sources. Now that you have completed a thorough study of your primary source, the Bible, refer to secondary sources. These include commentaries, concordances, atlases, Bible dictionaries and encyclopedias, theology books, and other reference works (again, refer to Appendix A). We must always use these tools with discernment because even godly people make mistakes. Some writers are more skilled than others, and all writers are influenced by their theological presuppositions or biases. It is helpful to know what an author's biases are (as well as your own) so you can glean what is good and leave the rest.

5. State your conclusions. Having consulted resources to help interpret your passage, state your conclusions. These should flow out of your work in the previous steps.

YOUR TURN

Try practicing just the first step of interpretation—stating an initial proposal (what you think the answer is). What do you think is the central message of Philippians 2:1-11?

Initial proposal:

In chapter 8 we will see what a complete interpretative study looks like. Then you will have an opportunity to do one of your own.

CHAPTER 8
The How To's of Interpretation

When I was asked a few years ago to head a missions organization, I felt awed by the responsibility of leadership. So I decided to study the Gospels to see how Jesus led people. As I gathered information I was struck by how much Jesus touched people in the course of His ministry. He touched Peter's mother-in-law (Mark 1:29-31), the leper (Luke 5:12-13), the dead girl and the woman with the hemorrhage (Matthew 9:18-25), and the man born blind (John 9:1-7). Though I had some initial ideas about what I would find, I began to realize that part of the Gospel writers' intended message was to show the compassion God has on us. I hadn't been looking for that but, as I studied the contexts of the passages and compared other Bible accounts, it impressed me so much that it changed the way I now function as a leader.

This chapter illustrates the process of interpretation mentioned above. It also provides opportunity to practice that process. Depending on what portion of Scripture you are studying, some areas of consideration will yield more fruit than others. For instance, in Philippians 2:1-11 you may have noticed that the question of *where* is not particularly illuminating. But if you were studying Exodus, location would be extremely significant.

The illustrations in this chapter use two passages: James 1 and Philippians 2. Both texts are provided because certain interpretation questions that are not helpful in one, are helpful in the other. Notice how the process of interpretation is done by following the principles outlined in chapter 7. You will have an opportunity to do the same type of research for Philippians 2:1-11 later in the chapter.

Observe Interpret Apply

Who? (the characters)
Find out all you can about the author and the recipients, including their identities and situations. If specific people or groups are mentioned, now is the time to learn more about them.

Example: James 1:1
Q: Who are the "twelve tribes" that were scattered abroad?

Initial proposal based on content: The twelve tribes must have been Jews who were living in many different places throughout the Roman Empire.

Context: James 2:2 refers to the "meeting" (NASB has "assembly") or synagogue (see margin note), not the church, which establishes the Jewish background of the group in question. However, this book is written to Christians (James 2:1), and therefore must be to converted Jews—Jewish Christians. James makes extensive use of Old Testament stories: 2:25; 5:11, 17. He also calls Abraham "our father" (2:21).

Comparison: Many early Christians were Jewish converts (Acts 1–7). Luke 22:30 uses the term "twelve tribes" to speak of Israel. John 7:35 refers to the Jews scattered among the Gentiles. Psalm 147:2; Isaiah 11:12; 56:8; and Zephaniah 3:10 also refer to this scattering of the Jews. This letter seems to have a special message for Christians who had problems specifically related to their Jewish backgrounds.

Consultation: Most commentators agree that James was written around A.D. 45 to Jewish converts scattered throughout the Roman Empire. H.A. Ironside, in his commentary, *James and Peter,* says, "The letter was addressed, not to any individual church or group of churches, as such, but to the twelve tribes of Israel in the Dispersion, those twelve tribes of whom Paul speaks in his address before Agrippa" (Acts 26:7).[1] This letter was circulated to these groups wherever they were found meeting in the old synagogues.

Conclusions: The twelve tribes scattered abroad are Jewish Christians facing unique challenges because of their heritage. They are located throughout the Roman Empire.

The How To's of Interpretation

What? (the key truths or events)
This is the time to investigate important words and ideas in the passage. What is the tone of the passage—joy, sorrow, disappointment, delight? If it is an action passage, what do the main actions represent?

Example: Philippians 2:1-3

Q. What does it mean to "Do nothing out of selfish ambition or vain conceit"?

Initial proposal based on content: Selfishness is usually caring more for yourself than for others. Conceit seems to imply useless or worthless vanity. From verses 2-4 it seems to mean a lack of unity, love, and purpose; the opposite of humility—pride; regarding yourself as more important than others; looking out for your own interests first.

Context: Paul is speaking here of the kind of conduct we in the church ought to exhibit (1:27). Christ is given as the great example of humility; He showed no selfishness or conceit. Notice also that Paul showed no selfishness in his lifestyle (1:22-26).

Comparison: Some of the Jewish Christians preached Christ out of selfish ambition (1:15-17), trying to harm Paul. Those who don't care about the good of the church are preaching the Gospel for their own gain. This selfish goal warrants the wrath of God and is a characteristic of unrighteousness (Romans 2:8). This ambition and conceit is contrary to the fruit of the Spirit (Galatians 5:25-26).

Consultation: The phrases *selfish ambition* and *vain conceit* mean "to be self-seeking" and are based on a false view of ourselves. A person with humility realizes his or her great dependence on God, and views others as equals before God. We are all equal in the church and should not put ourselves before others. Our dependence on God affects our behavior toward others.

Conclusions: Selfishness or conceit, as defined in this passage, is the opposite of humility. It is a self-seeking attitude that cares nothing about the welfare of the church, but only about the personal success of self.

Observe Interpret Apply

Where? (the geography and location)
Using the maps in your Bible or an atlas, locate where the author and readers were at the time of writing. Can you find all the places mentioned in the text? Can anything to be learned from the location of the events?

Example: James 1:1

Q. Where were these Jewish Christians of the Dispersion?

Initial proposal based on content: They could have been anywhere in the Roman Empire. The book of James tells us only that they were "scattered among the nations." A margin note translates the phrase literally as "the Dispersion"—a Greek term for a specific group of people.

Context: The book of James does not give us any help in locating them geographically.

Comparison: John 7:35 mentions the Dispersion, saying that they were among the Greeks. References from the Old Testament (noted in the *Who* study) tell us that these people are the remnant that were scattered abroad during the great Assyrian and Babylonian persecution. These Jews never returned to Israel when the nation was rebuilt under Ezra, Nehemiah, and Zerubbabel, but remained scattered throughout the Middle East (Psalm 147:2; Isaiah 11:12; 56:8; Zephaniah 3:10).

Consultation: Diaspora is the Greek word for "scattered," from which we get "dispersed." In New Testament times there were approximately 5 million Jews living outside of Palestine, scattered among the Greeks. They were descendants of all of the original twelve tribes of Israel. These communities of scattered Jews often became fertile soil for the spread of the Gospel. For example, Timothy's mother was a Jewish believer (Acts 16:1) who married a Greek living in Asia Minor.

Conclusions: The dispersed Jewish Christians were scattered throughout the Roman Empire wherever their descendants had settled after the Assyrian and Babylonian captivities.

The How To's of Interpretation

When? (the time factors)
Determine if there is anything critical related to the element of time in this passage. Does the message depend at all on certain aspects of the era in the church's history in which it was written? Are there lessons to be learned based on the timing of the events?

Example: Philippians 2:1-11

Q. Christ suffered before He gained victory; humiliation preceded exaltation. Is there a principle of timing here that is true for us?

Initial proposal based on content: This passage seems to teach that as Christians we too must suffer with Christ before we receive our reward of ultimate victory with Him in heaven. We should have the same attitude that Jesus had—that of humility. Jesus' exaltation was won through His humiliation on the cross.

Context: Philippians 1:29 says we will suffer as Christ did; Paul shares his own suffering and imprisonment in chapter 1. He also says that he lives on, not for himself, but for others. He seems to back up the humiliation of Christ—His suffering—with his own testimony. We too, it seems, are asked to live a life of humility, like both Paul and Jesus, before we can reign with Christ.

Comparison: Second Timothy 2:12 teaches that "if we endure, we will also reign with Him." Therefore, we will one day share His exaltation. We also know that Jesus taught that the greatest in the kingdom would serve all the others (John 13:12-15). Proverbs 18:12 says: "Before his downfall a man's heart is proud, but humility comes before honor." Serving is fundamental to reigning.

Consultation: John Calvin made the same observation about humility coming before victory: "He shows that abasement, to which the human mind is averse, is in the highest degree desirable—because everyone therefore who humbles himself will in like manner be exalted."[2]

Conclusions: There seems to be a biblical pattern about the progression from humiliation to exaltation. We must have the one before receiving the other. It could use further study, but the examples of Jesus and Paul support the principle.

Why? (the purpose of the passage or book)
The last task in interpreting Scripture is to discover the purpose of the passage. Remember, the purpose question is two-sided: there is the need that caused the revelation to be given, and there is the author's message which addressed that need. Here you are drawing conclusions based on all you have studied. To illustrate, look at the following example.

Example: James 1:1-18

▶ *The Need:* The readers of James seem to be in the midst of severe trials. Trials and temptations are the recurring needs mentioned in these eighteen verses.

▶ *The Message:* There are lessons to be learned and victories to be gained through trials, so look for the treasures behind the trials of life.

YOUR TURN

In this exercise, you will be going back to your work on pages 44–45 to apply the principles of interpretation to some of the questions you raised about Philippians 2:1-11. You may want to use additional paper for some of your research and Bible study. Your assignment is come up with one or more questions for each category: who, what, when, where. Then study through the steps of *content, context, comparison,* and *consultation* to arrive at *conclusions* regarding Philippians 2:1-11. You've seen a beginning of this work on pages 55 and 57. Now you can continue this work in more detail using the entire passage.

Pace yourself. This exercise will take approximately four hours to complete (45 minutes per section). You may choose to spend more time on some sections than others, depending on your particular areas of interest.

Be selective. There is not enough time in a day to do all the research in interpretation, so be selective. Choose one or two items to research and interpret in each of the areas—who, what, where, and when—then answer the question of why.

The How To's of Interpretation

WHO?

Research notes about people in Philippians 2:1-11

Observations	Questions	Answers
		Content: Context: Comparison: Consultation: Conclusion:

Observe Interpret Apply

WHAT?

Research notes about key truths of Philippians 2:1-11

Observations	Questions	Answers
		Content: **Context:** **Comparison:** **Consultation:** **Conclusion:**

The How To's of Interpretation

WHERE?

Research notes about significant geography, places, direction, or distance in Philippians 2:1-11

Observations	Questions	Answers
		Content: **Context:** **Comparison:** **Consultation:** **Conclusion:**

Observe Interpret Apply

WHEN?

Research notes about time in Philippians 2:1-11

Observations	Questions	Answers
		Content: Context: Comparison: Consultation: Conclusion:

The How To's of Interpretation

WHY?

We must deal with the question of *why* somewhat differently than the questions of *who, what, when* and *where*. When we ask *why* we must draw conclusions about the meaning of the passage, based on our study up to this point. Answer the following questions about Philippians 2:1-11 based on your findings and additional research.

1. Initial Proposal. Write an initial proposal to the twofold question of purpose.

▶ *The Reader's Needs:*

▶ *The Writer's Message:*

2. Context. What does the rest of the book of Philippians add to your understanding of the purpose of this passage—especially the material immediately before and after the passage?

Observe Interpret Apply

3. Comparison. How do cross-references, a concordance, and other translations, provide further insight on the purpose of Philippians 2:1-11? Where else does the Bible speak on this theme? How do these instances affect your understanding of this text?

4. Consultation. What do the experts say about the purpose of this passage or book? Write down several key comments from scholars that helped you understand the author's purpose in writing the text. (Refer to the list of resources in Appendixes A and B.)

The How To's of Interpretation

5. Conclusions. Having consulted other sources, now revise your initial proposal in light of any new insights. State your conclusion as a concise and personal interpretation of the passage.

▶ *The Reader's Needs:*

▶ *The Writer's Message:*

If you have filled the preceding pages with notes, you have now completed a thorough interpretation of Philippians 2:1-11, and have probably discovered a few new insights along the way. This is what makes Bible study exciting—at each level of investigation, God's Word yields great riches. Before moving on to the last stage of inductive Bible study, *application,* make a note here of two or three new aspects of Bible study that you learned from practicing *interpretation.* As a starting point, turn to the "possible answers" you wrote in the chart you created on pages 44–45. Have you enriched your understanding of those answers—or found entirely new ones? What other new insights have you discovered?

New Insights:

CHAPTER 9
Step 3: Application Asks, "How Will I Respond?"

I was brought up in a German Lutheran home. On Sundays I was an altar boy, but the rest of the week you'd never know it. My philosophy was that God graded on a curve, and if the good things I did outweighed the bad, that was good enough. I had no idea at that point what Paul meant when he said, "If anyone is in Christ, he is a new creation; the old has gone, the new has come!" (2 Corinthians 5:17) What I did on Sundays didn't apply to the rest of my life because I had not yet been made new in Christ; I was just going through the motions. Once I began to follow Christ, some changes had to take place.

All of your hard work in this book thus far has prepared you for the last step of inductive Bible study—*application*. You've gathered information, investigated the author's original meaning, and now you will be asking how to respond to what you have learned. Studying a rich passage like Philippians 2:1-11 no doubt brought a number of potential applications to mind. You may have already written several in your notes. Before we look at them, let's consider the importance of this last step in Bible study.

To stop without having applied what you have learned in your Bible study would be like cooking a sumptuous meal, serving it on fine china, and then walking away from the table without taking a bite! Just as eating is the goal of cooking, application, or obedience, is the goal of Bible study. It is the culmination of all your research. During the observation and interpretation stages you study the Word of God; in application, the Word of God studies you!

Step 3: Observation Asks, "How Will I Respond?"

Application: Putting Truths into Practice
Truth comes alive when it affects our personal experiences and circumstances. It is no coincidence that Jesus often chose to heal people *while* He proclaimed His Gospel of forgiveness. The reality of His message was expressed in changed lives. Martin Luther said:

> In truth thou canst not read the Scriptures too much;
> And what thou readest, thou canst not read too well;
> And what thou readest well, thou canst not too well understand;
> And what thou understandest well, thou canst not too well teach;
> And what thou teachest well, thou canst not too well live.[1]

What group of people was Jesus constantly confronting? Wasn't it the Pharisees? The Pharisees knew the letter of the law inside and out, but they failed to let it change their hearts. In condemning their hypocrisy, Jesus was saying that mere head knowledge of God's truths is not only not enough, it is in some ways worse than not having any. Think of His parable about the Good Samaritan (Luke 10:25-37). The very reason why the story stung the Pharisees and other religious leaders was because a Gentile Samaritan, a person without God's law, demonstrated more understanding of the intention of the law than the "professionals."

Too often Bible students resemble the Pharisees. We have more abstract knowledge of God than concrete experience with Him. Because greater obedience is the ultimate goal of Bible study, we need to make sure we are regularly applying the principles of Scripture to our lives.

One story tells of several pastors arguing about which Bible translation was best. One man startled the group by saying, "My grandmother's translation is the best I've ever read."

"What," his colleagues asked, "your grandmother translated the Bible?"

"Yes, she translated the Bible into her life, and it was the most powerful translation I've ever seen."

They got the point!

If we never apply the Scriptures to our lives, the Holy Spirit may eventually cease to reveal Himself to us. (Why should He continue to instruct those who don't want to obey Him?) The following exercise looks at a few key admonitions from the New Testament.

Observe Interpret Apply

YOUR TURN

Look up the Scripture references below and summarize what each passage teaches about the importance of application.

Matthew 7:24-27

John 8:31-32

James 1:22-25

A changed life is the clearest testimony of genuine understanding. Jesus said you can judge a tree by the fruit it bears (Matthew 7:15-18). But does everything in the Bible somehow apply to us? Do some things apply and not others, and if so, how can we know the difference?

Which of the following verses do you think apply to you today? If they do apply, would you apply them literally or generally? Explain your answer below.

The LORD had said to Abram, "Leave your country, your people and your father's household and go to the land I will show you."
— *Genesis 12:1*

☐ Applies directly ☐ Does not apply directly

Then Jesus came to them [the disciples] and said, "All authority in heaven and on earth has been given to Me. Therefore go and make disciples of all nations, baptizing them in the name of the Father and of the Son and of the Holy Spirit, and teaching them to obey everything I have commanded you. And surely I am with you always, to the very end of the age."
— *Matthew 28:18-20*

☐ Applies directly ☐ Does not apply directly

Step 3: Observation Asks, "How Will I Respond?"

All the believers were one in heart and mind. No one claimed that any of his possessions was his own, but they shared everything they had.
—Acts 4:32

☐ Applies directly   ☐ Does not apply directly

Now to the unmarried and the widows I [Paul] say: It is good for them to stay unmarried, as I am.
—1 Corinthians 7:8

☐ Applies directly   ☐ Does not apply directly

... women should remain silent in the churches. They are not allowed to speak, but must be in submission, as the Law says.
—1 Corinthians 14:34

☐ Applies directly   ☐ Does not apply directly

Dear friends, let us love one another, for love comes from God. Everyone who loves has been born of God and knows God.
—1 John 4:7

☐ Applies directly   ☐ Does not apply directly

For some of us, the thought of questioning whether or not a passage of the Bible applies to us today is unsettling. After all, doesn't 2 Timothy 3:16 say that "*All* Scripture is God-breathed and is useful for teaching, rebuking, correcting and training in righteousness"? How can we know what to apply to our situations?

Determining the Intended Audience
Before we apply a passage of Scripture, we must answer three questions:

☐ *Is this teaching local or universal?* Is the truth for a specific group at a specific location, or is it intended for everyone always?

☐ *Is the teaching temporary or timeless?* Is the truth to be applied in only a certain period of history, or is it always applicable?

☐ *What realm of experience does this passage speak to?* In what areas of our lives should we apply these truths?

To summarize, the basic principle of application is:

> Every teaching of Scripture should be received universally unless the Bible itself limits the audience, either in the context of the passage or other biblical teaching.

The Bible Sometimes Limits Itself
Keeping in mind the guideline above, the Bible does limit its application under at least two circumstances: *context* and *additional revelation*.

1. Context

☐ The context of a passage may indicate that it is not meant to be applied.

Example: In the book of Job, Elihu's "wisdom" is clearly not meant to be applied because it is contrary to the wisdom of God expressed later in the same book.

☐ The author may limit the application by addressing a specific group.

Example: In 1 Corinthians 7:8 Paul says it is better not to marry, but the text limits the application to those who have this "gift from God" (v. 7).

☐ A requirement that is clearly bound by the culture of that day may limit the application.

Example: The New Testament gives several warnings about not eating meat sacrificed to idols (Romans 14:21; 1 Corinthians 8:13; 10:28). Few cultures today have a similar situation. Unless you are a missionary, chances are you won't need to question the meat you are given to eat.

Step 3: Observation Asks, "How Will I Respond?"

[**Note:** Although history and culture may limit how we obey certain commands (like God's command to Abraham in Genesis 12:1), there is a place for applying universal principles within the passage. For example, we should follow Abraham's example of obeying God no matter what the cost.]

2. Additional Revelation
☐ New Testament revelation may limit how we are to apply some Old Testament Scriptures.

Example: Hebrews 9–10 teaches that the Levitical laws of the Old Covenant are no longer valid since the coming of Christ.

These principles are broadly defined by intention. Many of the specific questions you may have concerning how to apply a certain passage or book of the Bible are covered in the second half of this book. Part Two divides the books of the Bible according to genres, or types of literature, and each genre operates by slightly different rules of interpretation and application. For example, if you have a question on whether or how to apply a text from Matthew, refer to the chapter on Narratives. If you are not sure of the genre of your book, refer to the chart on page 83.

What are some of your questions about applying Scripture? Make a note of them here.

Questions about applying Scripture:

When you have completed this book, see if your questions have been answered—even if a specific question is not addressed, the list of study resources in Appendixes A and B can help you know where to look for the answer. Helpful books to consult for questions regarding interpretation or application are Gordon Fee and Douglas Stuart's *How to Read the Bible For All It's Worth* and Jack Kuhatschek's *Taking the Guesswork out of Applying the Bible*.

CHAPTER 10
In Application, God's Word Studies Us

As was mentioned at the end of chapter 9, many of the specific principles for applying Scripture are related to the genre or type of literature of the passage or book. These principles are discussed more fully in Part Two. In this chapter we will simply discuss four general guidelines for applying Scripture to your own life. Commit these to memory.

1. *Know yourself.* The better you know your own strengths and weaknesses, the more sensitive you will be to Scriptures that speak to your areas of need.

2. *Relate the passage to life.* Look for areas in your life where the principles you discover seem to apply the most.

3. *Meditate on the passage.* Reflecting on God's Word brings daily strength and wisdom as we seek to obey God.

4. *Practice what you have learned.* Discipline yourself to put the principles you have learned into practice.

Know Yourself
One way to know how to apply Scripture to your life is to know yourself well. Then, as you study the Bible you will find yourself saying, "Yes, I do tend to do _____" or "I do have a problem with _____." Perhaps you've never thought specifically

In Application, God's Word Studies Us

about the strengths and weaknesses in your walk with Christ. Because it can make a difference in how you personally appreciate and apply Scripture, take a moment here to list them. If you have a regular Bible study notebook or journal, keep the list there. Or use the space on this page. This is your own private list. You may want to add to it now and then as you discover more about yourself. Your list can help you to be alert to Scriptures that address those areas so that you can apply them specifically to your life.

YOUR TURN

Just for practice and to help you get started, begin a list of your strengths and weaknesses. (You may want to ask family and friends for their feedback.)

My Strengths:

My Weaknesses:

[**Note:** When studying Scripture in order to teach others, be aware of the characteristics and needs of your audience. Although you want to be sure to preach the whole Gospel, being sensitive to the concerns of your listeners will provide opportunities to bring the message home. Jesus often used people's personal needs as the context in which He proclaimed the Good News; He started with what was familiar to them and then challenged them to turn over their lives to God.]

Observe Interpret Apply

Relate the Passage to Life
As you were studying Philippians 2:1-11 through the steps of observation and interpretation, you probably discovered truths that seemed important for your life. That was the *purpose* for your study. Now it's time to summarize those truths into a principle statement. Throughout the Bible there are principles that speak directly to our lives. How are we to determine what those principles are? Here are three suggestions.

1. Write brief statements of universal truths that apply to you.

Examples:

From James 1:1-18: God uses trials to make us more mature. We can, therefore, have an attitude of joy in those trials, knowing that they have a purpose.

From Colossians 1:24-29: If I am trying to help someone grow in Christ, my goal is to see that person become like Christ—spiritually mature.

Once you have written a number of statements of application from a passage, you need to discern if they all apply to your situation.

2. Determine if the principle is timeless and universal.
A principle from Scripture is timeless and universal, unless the context itself, or subsequent Scripture limits it. Often, we do this part of application subconsciously while studying and writing applications. You probably wouldn't explore an application that did not apply to your situation. As an example of this reflex sort of thinking, turn to your responses to the questions on pages 68–69. Analyze why you decided that certain passages did not directly apply to you.

3. Look for new relationships.
Sometimes we need help in finding principles of application. One idea that may be useful is to see the Christian life as a series of new relationships. When attempting to apply the Bible, take a mental survey of your relationships. Then, open your life to potential change.

Take a moment right now to study the chart on page 75. Read it with your own network of relationships in mind asking God to show you areas where He wants to strengthen His work in your life. What did you discover? Jot a few notes in the space below.

NEW RELATIONSHIPS:

with God
- ☐ a truth to rest in
- ☐ a command to obey
- ☐ a prayer to express
- ☐ a challenge to heed
- ☐ a promise to trust
- ☐ a fellowship to enjoy

with yourself
- ☐ a thought or word to examine
- ☐ an action to take
- ☐ an example to follow
- ☐ an error to avoid
- ☐ an attitude to change or guard against
- ☐ a priority to change
- ☐ a goal to strive for
- ☐ a personal value or standard to hold up
- ☐ a sin to forsake

with others (home, church, work, school, society, world)
- ☐ a witness to share
- ☐ an encouragement to extend
- ☐ a service to do
- ☐ a forgiveness to ask
- ☐ a fellowship to nurture
- ☐ an exhortation to give
- ☐ a burden to bear
- ☐ a kindness to express
- ☐ a hospitality to extend
- ☐ an attitude to change or guard against
- ☐ a sin to renounce

with Satan
- ☐ a piece of spiritual armor to wear
- ☐ a temptation to resist
- ☐ a person to resist
- ☐ a sin to avoid and confess

Are there specific application principles that come to mind as you think of the passage in light of these relationships? If so, write them down in one-sentence statements.

Examples from James 1

(vv. 2-4) A truth to rest in: God uses trials in my life; they are no accident.

(vv. 6-8) An error to avoid: When trials come, I must be careful not to doubt God and lose my faith in Him. Rather, I need to seek God's help and wisdom in all of my trials.

(v. 12) A promise to trust: After I have endured the trials of life that God has allowed to come, I will receive a great reward from Him.

(vv. 12-18) A temptation to resist: When I am tempted, it is not God, but my own desire that is trying to pull me down. I should recognize this and ask for God's help, knowing that the temptation is in no way coming from Him.

Once you have discovered a number of application principles for your situation, then it is time to focus on one or two. Bring these focused principles to bear on specific situations in your life: your upcoming conversation with your son, your sense of worry as you anticipate a job change, what you will do with your free time on Saturday.

Meditate on the Passage

May my meditation be pleasing to Him, as I rejoice in the LORD.
— *Psalm 104:34*

It is a good idea to zero in on one key verse for application. In this way you can enjoy the fruit of your study throughout the day as you meditate on it. God promises rich reward to those who meditate on His Word:

Happy are those who do not follow the advice of the wicked,
   or take the path that sinners tread, or sit in the seat of scoffers;
but their delight is in the law of the LORD,
   and on his law they meditate day and night.
They are like trees planted by streams of water,
   which yield their fruit in its season, and their leaves do not wither.
In all that they do, they prosper.
— *Psalm 1:1-3* (NRSV)

In Application, God's Word Studies Us

Decide on one major point in the passage on which to focus, and memorize the verse in your passage that best expresses that principle.

Example from James 1:1-18

The key verse is verse 2: "Consider it pure joy, my brothers, whenever you face trials of many kinds." Think about what this verse says during the day and ask God to make it a part of your life.

Practice What You Have Learned

The last goal of Bible study and application is *action*. Although we can't always be diligently applying everything to our lives, we can consciously emphasize one or two at a time. Ask yourself, "What can I do?" Then write a specific action to take.

Example from James 1:18

I am going to practice listening to _____ at work and trying to understand her needs. Even though she frustrates me, I know that if I respond in the right way, God will use it to mature me—and possibly her, too.

YOUR TURN

Complete the application assignment below. Using the instructions in this chapter as a guide, develop application principles from Philippians 2:1-11, based on your work in the previous chapters. (Approximate time: 2–3 hours)

1. Know Yourself. You have already listed some areas that you consider to be your strengths and weaknesses. Do you see any ways in which the Philippians passage speaks to the items on your list? If so, simply list the ones that apply here.

2. *Relate the Passage to Life.* Based on what you've studied about writing application principles in this chapter, write at least six principles from Philippians 2:1-11 that seem to apply to you. Remember to keep application principles brief.

Are all the principles you listed timeless and universal? If so, go on to the next question. If not, write down what limits them.

Refer back to the list of relationships (p. 75). Do you see any other potential applications of the James passage for your life? If so, list them here.

In Application, God's Word Studies Us

3. Meditate on the Passage. Meditate both on the passage and the principles of application you have written. Select one verse in the passage to memorize and start working on that now. Then, single out one principle to emphasize from that verse and focus on it during the coming week. Write down the verse and the principle here.

Verse:

Principle:

4. Practice What You Have Learned. What will you *do* this week to apply these principles to your life? Based on your study of Philippians 2:1-11, write five concrete actions or attitudes you can work on this week.

You've now completed the three-step approach to inductive Bible study! You have put much hard work into getting to this point. Take a moment to reflect on what you have learned and on how you have grown. Pray that you may use your new skills to more faithfully handle the Word of Truth.

Part Two of this book takes the three steps and applies them to specific genres (types of literature) in Scripture. You will learn, for instance, the difference between studying a Gospel versus an epistle, how to interpret a psalm versus a prophetic book, and the way to appreciate Old Testament law now that Christ has come. The best is yet to come!

PART TWO

CHAPTER 11
How to Study a Whole Book of the Bible

Not all of Scripture is as simple and densely packed as the Book of Philippians. Genesis, for example, is fifty chapters of drama. (It's not possible to read Genesis five times in one sitting and write forty impressions—all in one comfortable evening of study.) Or how about the Book of Proverbs? Read any chapter in Proverbs and try to come up with one theme for the chapter or make a simple structural outline of it (see p. 37 for an example of a structural outline). It won't work. Proverbs is an altogether different genre, and must be studied somewhat differently than either Philippians or Genesis.

Different Genres, Different Concerns
In Part One you studied the general principles of inductive Bible study, with plenty of opportunities to practice those steps. Building on these fundamentals, you will now apply the steps to different books of the Bible. Because there are several kinds of literature in Scripture (poetry, prose, parables, and others), we need to know what types of questions to ask or concerns to be aware of for each kind of literature.

Each time we look at a new kind of biblical literature, or genre, we will list all the books that fall into that particular category and note some of the unique features of that genre as well as general principles for proper interpretation of that genre. Just as in Part One, you will be given opportunities to practice how to *observe, interpret,* and *apply* each type of biblical book.

Leland Ryken, in *The Literature of the Bible,* expresses well the unique variety of the Scriptures.

> Biblical literature is a collection or anthology of works written by a variety of writers over the span of many centuries. The very title "Bible" means "little books." Biblical literature is a small library containing a survey of Hebraic-Christian literature as it was written over a long period of time. . . .
>
> The fact that biblical literature is an anthology results in a remarkable variety of forms and styles. Literary forms represented in the Bible include the story of origins, heroic narrative, epic, parody, tragedy, lyric, epithalamion (wedding poem), encomium (high praise), wisdom literature, proverb, parable, pastoral, satire, prophecy, Gospel, epistle, oratory and apocalypse.[1]

But don't let the variety of literary forms discourage or confuse you. God has chosen to use many different and creative ways to communicate His message to us, and we can thank Him for this richness.

Scholars typically divide the different types of biblical literature into five major categories with some books appearing in more than one classification. These categories are: *narrative, epistle, wisdom literature, poetry,* and *prophecy.*

Why Study a Whole Book?
When Paul wrote to the church at Philippi, he penned a letter, not a series of fragmented sentences. When Moses recorded all of the dramatic movements Israel made in the journey from Egypt to the border of Canaan, he wrote the Book of Exodus. Though we often pick out favorite verses from Scripture to teach or to memorize, we need to understand the whole book (the context) in order for its parts to make sense.

This kind of Bible study is a "telescope approach," because we begin by standing back and looking at the book in its entirety. Once we have understood the structure and message of the book as a whole, the meaning of the individual parts becomes more clear. Perhaps the most common reason people misunderstand, misinterpret, and therefore, misuse Scripture is because they fail to study a passage in the context of its entire surroundings. Sound interpretation is based on defining each verse within its context; the largest context in which to define each verse is the whole book. So the logical place to begin Bible study is by looking at whole books of Scripture.

One of the most important tools for studying a book of the Bible is the *book chart.* This text will ask that you make a chart each time you observe an entire book. These charts will come in handy in the future when you reread and study the same books. You can gain a great deal from making your own book chart, rather than looking at what someone else

> ## FIVE KINDS OF BIBLICAL LITERATURE
>
> **Narrative:**
>
> *Old Testament:* Genesis, Exodus, Leviticus, Numbers, Deuteronomy, Joshua, Judges, Ruth, 1 and 2 Samuel, 1 and 2 Kings, 1 and 2 Chronicles, Ezra, Nehemiah, Esther, Daniel, Jonah, Haggai
>
> *New Testament:* Matthew, Mark, Luke, John, Acts
>
> **Epistle:**
>
> Romans, 1 and 2 Corinthians, Galatians, Ephesians, Philippians, Colossians, 1 and 2 Thessalonians, 1 and 2 Timothy, Titus, Philemon, Hebrews, James, 1 and 2 Peter, 1, 2, and 3 John, Jude
>
> **Wisdom Literature:**
>
> Job, Proverbs, Ecclesiastes
>
> **Poetry:**
>
> Psalms, Song of Solomon
>
> **Prophecy and Revelation:**
>
> *Major Prophets:* Isaiah, Jeremiah, Lamentations, Ezekiel, Daniel
>
> *Minor Prophets:* Hosea, Joel, Amos, Obadiah, Jonah, Micah, Nahum, Habakkuk, Zephaniah, Haggai, Zechariah, Malachi
>
> Revelation

has already done. Irving Jensen stresses the importance of discovering the book's structure for yourself:

> James M. Gray, who pioneered in the developing and teaching of the book survey method of study, maintained rightly that one's own original and independent study of the broad pattern of a book in the Bible, imperfect as the conclusions may be, is of far more value to the student than the most perfect outline obtained from someone else. This is not to minimize the work of others, but to emphasize that recourse to outside aids should be made only after the student has taken his own skyscraper view.[2]

Noticing the arrangement of the parts of a book—finding its structure—opens up the meaning and intention of the author. Structure is what unifies the book and holds it together. It is like the frame of a house on which the doors and walls are hung. In chapter 5 you made a structural outline and looked for the principles of structure in Philippians 2:1-11. With an entire book of Scripture, however, you cannot make the same type of structural outline—time and space simply don't allow it. A more effective way of understanding the structure of a book is to make a chart.

All of the lessons in Part Two follow the three-step inductive approach:

1. Observe the facts
2. Interpret your findings
3. Apply the truth

You may find that at times you need more explanation of the inductive approach than is provided. Refer back to the appropriate section in Part One with any questions you have about how to observe, interpret, or apply the Bible. For those who would like more information about how to study particular genres of Scripture, Gordon Fee and Douglas Stuart's book, *How to Read the Bible for All It's Worth* is an excellent resource.

Let's begin our study of whole books of the Bible by starting with a familiar type—*narratives*.

CHAPTER 12
Narratives—True Stories about God and His People

I've spent a lot of my life waiting. Perhaps you feel the same. When I read about how God was faithful to other people in history, people like Moses, or Joseph, or Daniel—people who waited a long time for God to fulfill His promises—I am encouraged. It's one reason why I love the narrative books of the Bible; they are stories about people like you and me and the God who watched over them.

We begin our study of whole books of the Bible with narratives because more than half the Bible is narrative. Over 40 percent of the Old Testament and 65 percent of the New Testament is stories. What is a *narrative*?

Narratives are material that relate the history of an era in a narrative manner—telling how God worked in a certain time and allowing us to hear the characters of history speak. The following books are included in the category of *narrative*: (Daniel, Jonah, and Haggai appear here and also under prophecy.)

Old Testament			New Testament
Genesis	Judges	Nehemiah	Matthew
Exodus	Ruth	Esther	Mark
Leviticus	1 and 2 Samuel	Daniel	Luke
Numbers	1 and 2 Chronicles	Jonah	John
Deuteronomy	1 and 2 Kings	Haggai	Acts
Joshua	Ezra		

Observe Interpret Apply

Special Features of Narratives
Since narratives comprise so much of the Bible, some of your favorite stories are probably from historical sections of the Bible. For example, it's in the Gospels that we read the historical account of the incarnation, ministry, crucifixion, resurrection, and ascension of Jesus Christ. The Book of Acts deals with the birth of the church. Some of us as young children learned to appreciate the Christian heritage of our parents and Sunday School teachers through this historical material. Stories of heroes like David, who killed the giant Goliath, and Daniel, whose God closed the mouths of the lions, made the Bible come alive for us.

In their book *How to Read the Bible for All It's Worth,* Gordon Fee and Douglas Stuart summarize what biblical narratives are and what they are not. Consider these important points.

1. Old Testament narratives are not just stories about people who lived in Old Testament times. They are first and foremost stories about what God did to and through those people. In contrast to human narratives, the Bible is composed especially of divine narratives. God is the hero of the story—if it is in the Bible. Characters, events, developments, plot, and story climaxes all occur, but behind these, God is the supreme "protagonist" or leading decisive character in all narratives.

2. Old Testament narratives are not allegories or stories filled with hidden meanings. But there may be aspects of narratives that are not easy to understand. We are often not told precisely all that God did in a certain situation that caused it to happen the way the Old Testament reports it. And even when we are told what He did, we are not always told how or why He did it. . . .

3. Old Testament narratives do not always teach directly. They emphasize God's nature and revelation in special ways that legal or doctrinal portions of the Bible never can, by allowing us vicariously to live through events and experiences rather than simply learning about the issues involved in those events and experiences. Narratives thus give you a kind of "hands on" knowledge of God's work in His world, and though this knowledge is secondary rather than primary, it is nevertheless a real knowledge that can help shape your behavior. . . .

4. Each individual narrative or episode within a narrative does not necessarily have a moral all its own. Narratives cannot be interpreted atomistically, as if every statement, every event, every description could, independently of the others, have a special message for the reader. In fact, even in fairly lengthy narratives all the component parts of the narrative can work together to impress upon the reader a single major point. There is an overall drift or movement to a narrative, a kind of superstructure that makes the point, usually a single point.[1]

Having laid some of the groundwork for understanding what narratives are and are not, let's begin to study them inductively. In Part Two it is assumed that you have completed

Narratives—True Stories about God and His People?

the information and practice studies in Part One, where the three steps of inductive study are discussed in full. If you need more information on the inductive approach than is given in these next chapters, refer back to Part One and review the process.

Observing Narratives
Our first task is to observe the facts that make up that book. Remember, when we study whole books of the Bible we do not look at minute details; we are working toward a broad understanding of the book's teaching. We will use the Book of 1 Samuel for our sample study and the Gospel of John for the work in "Your Turn."

Observing the Whole
1. Read the book carefully. This is the first essential in observing a book. For some books this is easier than others. As was noted earlier, reading through the Book of Philippians goes more quickly than Genesis (50 chapters) or Acts (28 chapters).

This initial reading of the entire book gives you a general overview of its contents, including the major characters, events, and themes. When reading a longer book of the Bible (which many of the historical books are), you can take one of two approaches: (1) skim the book, reading only for broad content; or (2) read it in a few sittings.

For this study, we suggest that you skim the Gospel of John in one reading, looking only for the big picture.

2. Record your initial impressions. Record your initial observations as you read along. Only record the broad facts about:

> **Who?** (the major characters)
> **What?** (the major events and themes)
> **Where?** (the major locations)
> **When?** (the major divisions of time)

After looking over the sample of 1 Samuel on page 88, complete "Your Turn." But first, page through the book of John and make a few notes about your overall impression. Use the space below. Then record your detailed observations on pages 89-90.

Observe Interpret Apply

Example: 1 Samuel

The following list of first impressions was made while reading the Book of 1 Samuel. These are sample observations; a complete list would fill many pages.

Who?

The major characters in the drama are Eli, Samuel, Saul, and David.

What?

1. Samuel is the last judge of Israel.
2. Preparation is being made for the first king of the nation.
3. Saul becomes the first king.
4. Saul does not make a good king and commits many sins.
5. David is chosen as king but does not become king.
6. Much of the action is the conflict between the two key characters: Saul and David.
7. Throughout the last half of the book, David runs from a jealous King Saul.
8. Saul dies a horrible death at the end of the book.
9. David is the hero of the book, Saul the villain.

Where?

1. All the events take place in and around Palestine.
2. The action starts at Shiloh.
3. There is much geographical movement because of wars and Saul's pursuit of David.

When?

1. The action takes places over many years.
2. It is a time of transition for Israel, moving from the days of the Judges to rule by a king.
3. Saul reigns for thirty-three years, all of which are recorded in 1 Samuel.
4. David flees for many years, not just a few months!
5. First Samuel records David's early years, before his kingship.

Narratives — True Stories about God and His People?

YOUR TURN

Spend some time observing the Gospel of John. As you skim through John, jot down your initial observations concerning who, what, where, and when. (Don't wait until after you've read the whole book to record your observations — you will have forgotten too much by then.) Remember to keep your observations general; now is not the time to get bogged down in details. (Approximate time: 90 minutes)

Who?

What?

Observe Interpret Apply

Where?

When?

Observing the Parts
Studying the structure of an entire book of Scripture reveals the design of the author, who is both the human writer and God Himself. In this phase of observation we will chart a book of Scripture and look for the principles of structure in that book. Irving Jensen's book, *Independent Bible Study,* is probably the best book available on chartmaking in Bible study. Jensen devotes much of his book to teaching how to produce charts of the Bible. On the next page is an example of a chart created from a study of the Book of Acts.

Narratives—True Stories about God and His People?

ACTS: 35 YEARS OF EARLY CHURCH HISTORY

A.D. 29							33				45																60-62
EAST	TAKEN UP	HOLY SPIRIT	GATE BEAUTIFUL	ARREST	LIE	WIDOWS	STEPHEN	PHILIP	SAUL	CORNELIUS	PETER	HEROD	CYPRUS & ANTIOCH	LYSTRA & DERBE	JERUSALEM COUNCIL	PHILIPPI 15:36	ATHENS	CORINTH	EPHESUS 18:23	FAREWELL	JERUSALEM ARREST	STAIRWAY 21:17	PLOT	FELIX	FESTUS	AGRIPPA	SHIPWRECK	ROME	WEST
	1	2	3	4	5	6	7	8:1b	9	10	11	12	13	14	15		17		19	20		22	23	24	25	26	27	28
	BIRTH OF CHURCH		GROWTH THROUGH TESTING					GREAT PERSECUTION		GOSPEL TO GENTILES			1ST JOURNEY			2ND JOURNEY			3RD JOURNEY			JERUSALEM			CAESAREA			TO ROME
	JERUSALEM							JUDEA & SAMARIA					ENDS OF EARTH														
	CHURCH ESTABLISHED							CHURCH SCATTERED					CHURCH EXTENDED														
	JEWISH PERIOD							TRANSITION					GENTILE PERIOD														

Key Verse: 1:8
Key Word: "Witness"
Author: Luke
Date Written: A.D. 61-64

Taken from *Independent Bible Study*, by Irving L. Jensen. Copyright 1979, Moody Bible Institute of Chicago. Moody Press. Used by permission.

Use this chart as a guide when you make your chart of the Gospel of John. The first time around it probably won't look as refined as Irving Jensen's chart on Acts, but soon you will be producing the same kinds of results. When charting a book, you may go through several revisions. Your first chart might be nothing more than an array of facts scattered over the page. Subsequent revisions will help you simplify and emphasize the major elements of the book.

The blank chart on page 92 shows how to lay out a study sheet for this type of exercise. Whenever you study a whole book of the Bible, start by making a chart like this one, with enough boxes for all the chapters. Some books, like Genesis, will take several pages. As you read, make brief notes of the major contents of each chapter. (You may want to think of a short title for each paragraph in the chapter.) Then fill in the chapter section of your chart with a chapter title that summarizes or reflects the contents of that chapter. At the bottom of the chart you could also note the key verse and key word in the chapter. As your understanding of the book's structure grows, you can add more information. The chart on page 93 is an example of a refined chart of the Book of Jonah. Two sample charts on pages 94–95 are provided for the Book of 1 Samuel. The first chart is a first draft chart of 1 Samuel. (Some of the principles of structure are marked on the chart.) The information from the draft chart was then refined and sifted down into the second, summary chart on page 96. Spend some time studying these charts.

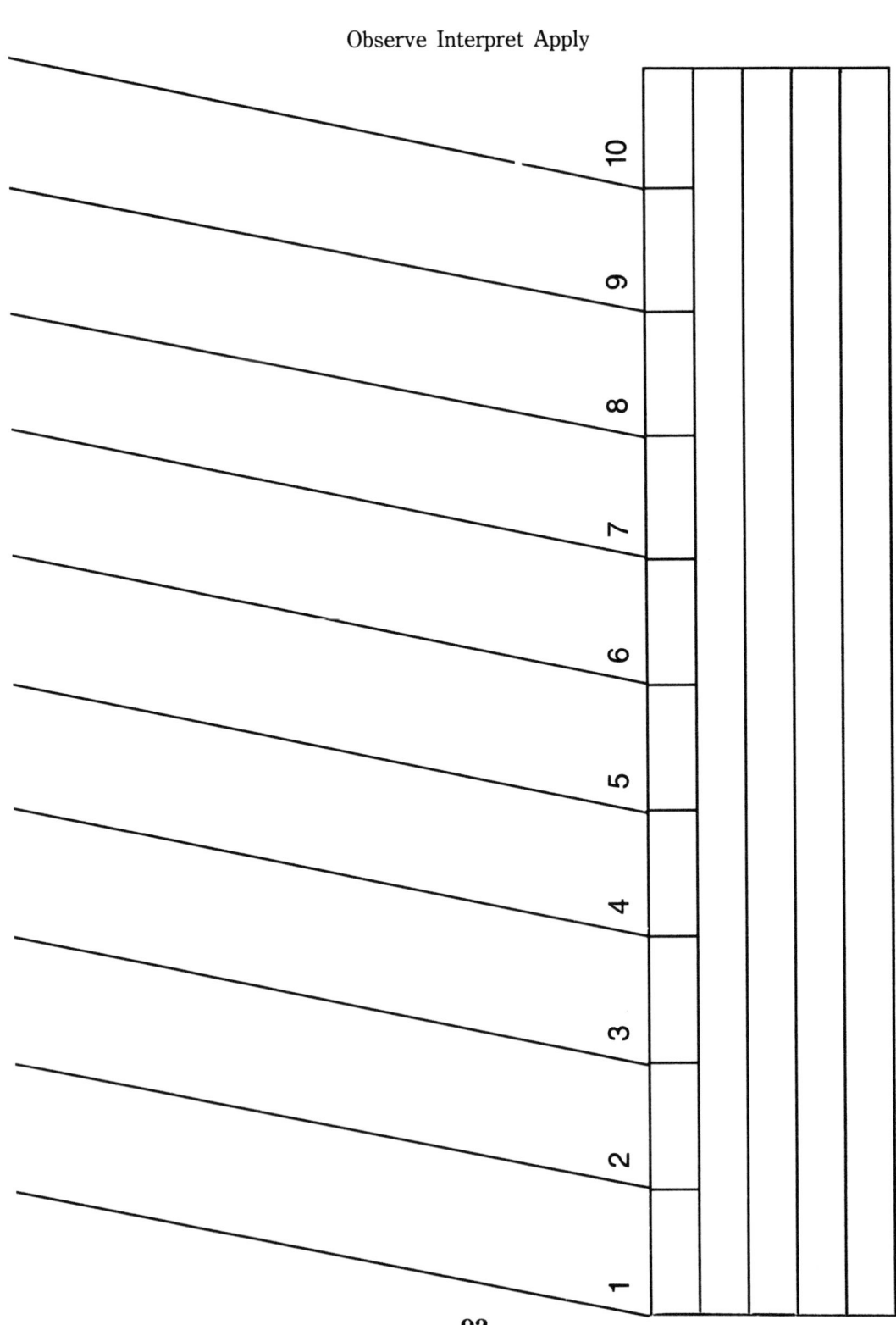

Narratives—True Stories about God and His People?

THE BOOK OF JONAH

	JONAH'S FIRST COMMISSION CHAPTERS 1-2			JONAH'S SECOND COMMISSION CHAPTERS 3-4		
DISOBE-DIENCE	CHASTISEMENT	PRAYER		OBE-DIENCE	BLESS-ING	PRAYER

1:1	1:4	1:10	1:15	1:17	2:10	3:1	3:5	3:10	4:5	4:9
DISOBEDIENCE OF JONAH TO COMMISSION	STORM AND THE DISCOVERY OF ITS CAUSE	ATTEMPT OF SAILORS TO SAVE JONAH	CASTING OF JONAH INTO THE SEA	PRAYER OF JONAH INSIDE FISH	DELIVERANCE OF JONAH FROM FISH	OBEDIENCE OF JONAH TO COMMISSION	REPENTANCE OF NINEVEH	PRAYER OF JONAH OUTSIDE NINEVEH	DEALING OF GOD WITH JONAH	APPEAL BY GOD TO JONAH

From the book *How to Study the Bible*, by James Braga. 1982 by Multnomah Press. Portland, Oregon 97266. Used by permission.

CHART OF 1 SAMUEL

	ELI				SAMUEL					SAUL				
						SAMUEL'S DAY AS THE LAST JUDGE OF ISRAEL				SAMUEL'S FAREWELL SPEECH AS LEADER			SAUL (AS KING)	LOSES DIVINE AUTHORITY
ELKANAH & HANNAH & PENINNAH	HANNAH'S SONG OF PRAISE	SAMUEL MEETS LORD IN VISION	ISRAEL FIGHTS PHILISTINES	ARK TO ASHDOD TO BE PUT BY DAGON	PHILISTINES RETURN ARK TO ISRAEL	ARK TO KIRJATH-JEARIM	SAMUEL OLD, SONS BECOME JUDGES; DON'T FOLLOW LORD	SAUL, SON OF KISH SEEKS FOR LOST DONKEYS	SAUL ANOINTED BY SAMUEL	JABESH ATTACKED BY AMMONITES	SAMUEL ADDRESSES ALL ISRAEL	WAR WITH PHILISTINES BEGINS	JONATHAN WINS A GREAT VICTORY FOR ISRAEL	SAUL SENT TO DEFEAT AMALEKITES
HANNAH PRAYS FOR SON	ELI'S SONS SIN	ELI'S DOOM TOLD	LOSES; ARK STOLEN; ELI'S SONS KILLED	ARK TO GATH TO EKRON	TO BETH-SHEMESH	ELEAZAR CONSECRATED TO KEEP ARK	PEOPLE ASK FOR A KING	GOES TO INQUIRE OF SAMUEL & IS TREATED AS ROYALTY	PROPHESY & HIS RETURN TO PROPHETIC MINISTRY	SAUL HEARS & DRAWS ISRAEL TOGETHER TO FIGHT	REMINDS THEM OF PAST SINS & GOD'S PATIENCE	SAUL'S GREAT SIN #1—OFFERING THE BURNT OFFERING	JONATHAN ACCIDENT-ALLY EATS HONEY BUT IS DELIVERED FROM DEATH	SAUL SINS BY KEEPING SPOILS #2
SAMUEL BORN	SONS & SAMUEL CONTRASTED DOOM OF ELI'S HOUSE TOLD	SAMUEL GROWS & CONFIRMED AS PROPHET	ELI HEARS & DIES 40-YEAR MINISTRY ENDS	AFFLICTION BY GOD ON EACH PLACE	MANY SLAIN BY LORD BECAUSE THEY DEFILED THE ARK	SAMUEL GATHERS ALL OF ISRAEL, LEADERS TO MIZPAH	LORD SAYS OK BUT THEY'LL BE SORRY		SAUL PROPHESIES	GREAT VICTORY IS WON	TELLS THEM OF THEIR GREAT SIN IN ASKING FOR A KING	SAMUEL RETURNS & DISCOVERS SAUL'S SIN	WARS AGAINST MANY & SAUL'S VICTORIES	GOD REJECTS SAUL AS KING; SAMUEL WORRIES
GIVEN TO LORD AT SHILOH & TO ELI	SAMUEL'S PROPHECY		ICHABOD BORN TO PHINEHAS' WIFE			REVIVAL	PEOPLE HARD; STILL WANT A KING		SAUL CHOSEN BY LOT TO BE KING	SAUL MADE KING!	FEAR THE LORD & SERVE HIM WITH ALL YOUR HEARTS!	ISRAEL OPPRESSED BY PHILISTINES		LORD GRIEVED OVER SAUL
			GLORY HAS GONE!			VICTORY OVER PHILISTINES								
1	2	3	4	5	6	7	8	9	10	11	12	13	14	15

PREPARATION OF SAMUEL | DEFEAT → 7 MOS. | VICTORY | SAUL CHOSEN AS KING < NOT WHAT GOD WANTED | VICTORY (SORT OF) | ▽ Pivot SAUL'S LEADERSHIP BEGINS | WARS →

SAUL 40 YRS. OLD

Bulk of Samuel's life

SAMUEL—PROPHET —JUDGE —PRIEST (9)

Continued on next page.

94

16	17	18	19	20	21	22	23	24	25	26	27	28	29	30	31
LORD SENDS SAMUEL TO FIND NEW KING	PHILISTINES WAR WITH ISRAEL	JONATHAN & DAVID KNIT	SAUL'S ATTEMPTS CONTINUE; DAVID SAVED BY JONATHAN & MICHAL	JONATHAN & DAVID RELATE	FLEES TO NOB TO AHIMELECH THE PRIEST	FLEES TO CAVE OF ADULLAM & GATHERS MEN	DAVID SAVES KEILAH IN VICTORY	SAUL PURSUES DAVID AT ENGEDI WITH 3,000 TROOPS	SAMUEL DIES	SAUL PURSUES DAVID AT ZIPH WITH 3,000 TROOPS	DAVID FLEES TO PHILISTINES & GETS ZIKLAG AS HIS CITY	PHILISTINES GATHERED TO FIGHT ISRAEL	ARMIES GATHERED TO FIGHT	ZIKLAG DESTROYED BY AMALEKITES	ISRAEL DEFEATED BY PHILISTINES
DAVID, SON OF JESSE, PICKED AS KING	GOLIATH PREVAILS	DAVID PROSPERS	DAVID'S FLIGHT FROM SAUL BEGINS; TEAMS UP WITH SAMUEL	JONATHAN DISCOVERS SAUL'S HATRED FOR DAVID	EATS BREAD & LIES	SAUL INQUIRES OF AHIMELECH & ACCUSES THEM OF SITTING BY DAVID	SAUL PURSUES DAVID AT KEILAH & DAVID & HIS MEN FLEE	DAVID SPARES SAUL'S LIFE IN CAVE	NABAL TREATS DAVID'S MEN BADLY	DAVID SPARES SAUL'S LIFE AGAIN	DAVID LEADS RAIDS FOR PHILISTINES	SAUL SCARED & SEEKS A MEDIUM	DAVID IS NOT TRUSTED AND IS FORCED TO RETURN WITH HIS MEN TO LAND OF PHILISTINES	DAVID & COMPANY PURSUE & DEFEAT AMALEKITES	SAUL & SONS SLAIN
LORD LEAVES SAUL & EVIL SPIRIT COMES	ISRAEL FEAR'S DAVID'S FAITH!	SAUL JEALOUS & PLOTS FOUR TIMES TO KILL DAVID		JONATHAN & DAVID COVENANT TOGETHER & PART COMPANY	FLEES TO GATH & KING ACHISH & ACTS INSANE	85 PRIESTS ARE KILLED & DAVID MOURNS		DAVID & SAUL TALK & COME TO AGREEMENT	DAVID PLOTS TO KILL	DAVID & SAUL PART WAYS	ACHISH PLEASED	SAMUEL TELLS OF SAUL'S DOOM		SPOILS BROUGHT TO ELDERS OF JUDAH	SAUL'S HEAD DISPLAYED & THEN RESCUED
DAVID SOOTHES SAUL'S TROUBLES	GOLIATH SLAIN BY DAVID; ALL OF ISRAEL REJOICES	DAVID MARRIES MICHAL & PROSPERS GREATLY	SAUL PROPHESIES						ABIGAIL INTERCEDES & DAVID STOPS			SAUL DISPARES OF LIFE			
									NABAL LED BY LORD						
									DAVID WEDS ABIGAIL						

Biographical & chronological progression: the stories of three men!

— KEEPS SINNING →   DAVID FLEES FROM SAUL   DAVID WITH PHILISTINES →

DAVID

PIVOT — SAUL JEALOUS OF DAVID (v. 9) — Faith / Fear

KEY TO SAUL'S HATRED: 20:31 → 23:17 → 24:20

400 MEN → 600 MEN

Ends in defeat

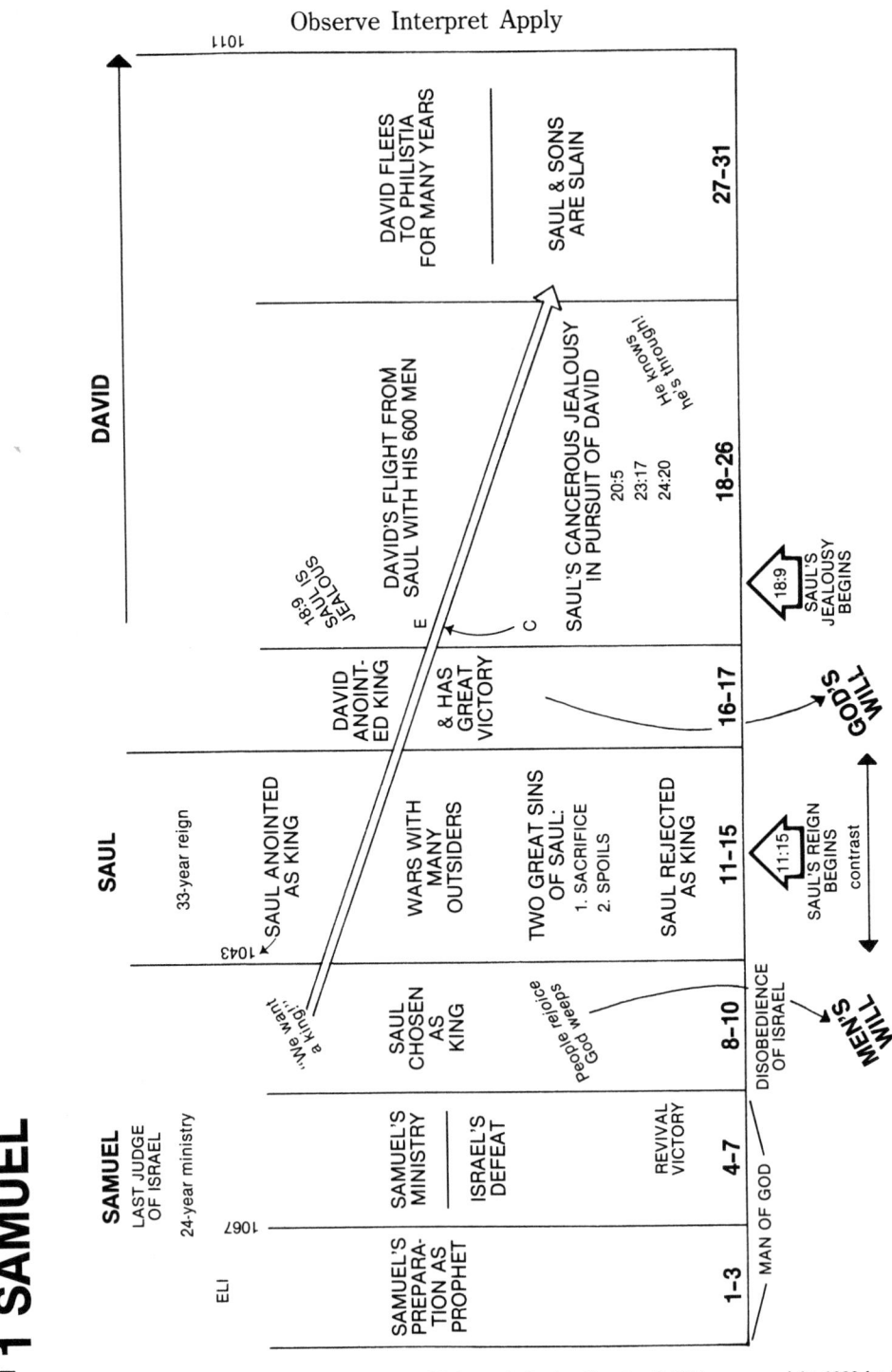

Narratives—True Stories about God and His People?

Now you'll have an opportunity to try the technique of book charting on the Gospel of John. But before you do, review the principles of structure which are defined and explained in Appendix C.

YOUR TURN

On the following pages, draw a book chart for the Gospel of John, allowing enough space for all 21 chapters. Then begin reading through John. As you read, jot down brief notes about the major facts of each chapter, perhaps coming up with a paragraph title for each chapter. This is the most important part of your Bible study and will take the most time. Once you've completed your first draft, go back and refine your information. Include and mark the patterns of structure explained in Appendix C. Then sift the information in your first draft chart down to a final, summary chart. (Approximate time: 2 hours)

BOOK CHART OF THE GOSPEL OF JOHN
First draft

BOOK CHART OF THE GOSPEL OF JOHN
Continued first draft

BOOK CHART OF THE GOSPEL OF JOHN
Final draft

Interpreting Narratives

Interpretation asks: "What is God trying to teach through this account of history?" But,

> An event or specific behavior should not be considered normative for today solely on the basis that it is recorded in the Bible. It must be evaluated in the light of direct biblical teaching. . . .
>
> A historical event always has some implication. Otherwise, it would not be included in Holy Writ. And often there is more than one implication. A general principle may be inferred from a historic event that is interpreted by Scripture. If an event is not interpreted by Scripture, it may not be used to derive a doctrine or principle of conduct.
>
> Scripture leaves many historic events uninterpreted, but of many it renders a judgment: the behavior is either commended or condemned. In some of those instances Scripture goes even further; it gives a reason for the commendation or condemnation. Such interpreted events are the legitimate raw material for refining general principles.[2]

Fee and Stuart list ten principles to keep in mind when interpreting narratives.

PRINCIPLES FOR INTERPRETING NARRATIVES

1. An Old Testament narrative usually does not directly teach a doctrine.
2. An Old Testament narrative usually illustrates a doctrine or doctrines taught propositionally elsewhere.
3. Narratives record what happened—not necessarily what should have happened or what ought to happen every time. Therefore, not every narrative has an individual identifiable moral of the story.
4. What people do in narratives is not necessarily a good example for us. Frequently, it is just the opposite.
5. Most of the characters in the Old Testament narratives are far from perfect and their actions are too.
6. We are not always told at the end of a narrative whether what happened was good or bad. We are expected to be able to judge that on the basis of what God has already taught us directly and categorically in the Scripture.
7. *All* narratives are selective and incomplete. Not all the relevant details are always given (John 21:25). What does appear in the narrative is everything that the inspired author thought important for us to know.
8. Narratives are not written to answer all our theological questions. They have particular, specific limited purposes and deal with certain issues, leaving others to be dealt with elsewhere, in other ways.
9. Narratives may teach either explicitly (by clearly stating something) or implicitly (by clearly implying something without actually stating it).
10. In the final analysis, God is the hero of all biblical narratives.[3]

Narratives — True Stories about God and His People?

New Testament narratives have some of the same features as Old Testament narratives, but are unique in several ways because the Gospels record the life and ministry of Jesus Christ.

> The Gospels are collections of stories, far more packed with action than is customary in narrative. The overriding purpose of the Gospel stories is to explain and praise the person and work of Jesus, who is always the moving force behind the writers' presentation. The impulse to get the facts of Jesus' life and meaning before the reader is combined with the impulse to celebrate what is recorded. The person and work of Jesus are presented through several narrative devices — through His actions, through His words, and through the responses of other people to Him.[4]

When interpreting the Gospels specifically, always look at their teachings in relation to the person of Jesus Christ. Ask, "How does this story — these events — relate to Jesus Christ and my response to Him?"

When interpreting narratives, we want to focus on the broader question of *why*. It is in answering the *why* question that we discover the purpose for the book, which includes the need that caused the revelation to be given and the author's *message* which addressed that need.

> ▶ *The Need.* All narrative books of the Bible fill a basic need: they record how God responded in history to the needs of His people by directly intervening in their lives. Because each book fills that need, it is not necessary to look for specific needs in the era itself. It *is* necessary, however, to look for the specific message of the book.

> ▶ *The Message.* Look for the core truth of the book. Ask, "What is the underlying message or theme of this book?" Then ask, "What solutions or information does the author give to meet the needs of his readers?" Try to determine the unique contribution the book is making to the canon of Scripture. Then summarize in one sentence the message of the entire book. Simply stated, this is your initial proposal of what you think is the message.

You can formulate the answers to the question of why by looking in the same places we always look: *content, context, comparison,* and *consultation* of secondary sources. Finally, you can make your *conclusion* based on your findings.

1. State your initial proposal based on the content. First and foremost, your interpretation should arise out of the book you are studying, not out of what someone else has said it means. Always begin with the Bible as your primary source.

2. Search the context. The context of narrative books includes other biblical books of the same immediate era in history. What, for example, does 2 Samuel add to your understanding of 1 Samuel? Do other books add to your understanding of the message? (For example, the book of Ruth tells the story of David's great grandmother.)

3. Seek comparison. The Bible itself sheds light on its own meaning. Sound interpretation takes into account the corporate teaching of Scripture. What do cross-references, other narrative books, and other translations add to your understanding of this book? Are segments of this book quoted, referred to, or commented on in other parts of Scripture?

4. Survey/Consult secondary sources. Once you have completed a thorough study of your primary source—the Bible—consult resources for help (commentaries, atlases, Bible dictionaries, theology books). It is always helpful to check your own statements about a book's purpose and message with what scholars have to say about it.

5. State your conclusions. Having consulted all necessary resources to help you in your interpretation, modify your initial proposal to reflect your new insights.

Example: 1 Samuel

The Book of 1 Samuel has a specific message. It records the official account of the end of the period of the theocracy under the judges, and shows the foundation of the monarchy under the new system of rule by kings. Under the monarchy, sin continued to hamper God's best for His people and had political and personal consequences.

Now try your hand at interpreting the Gospel of John.

YOUR TURN

Write an interpretive statement which summarizes what you believe is the primary message of the Gospel of John. Having spent time charting John, you already have a good idea of what the book is about. Now make an initial proposal as to the message of the book, and go through the other steps for finding the answers for interpretation.

WHY
1. State your initial proposal based on the content. Based on your study of John up to this point, what do you *think* is the message or theme of the book? State your proposal in one or two sentences.

Narratives—True Stories about God and His People?

2. Search the context. The context of the Gospel of John is the other Gospel accounts: Matthew, Mark, and Luke. How do the other Gospels add to your understanding of the message of John?

3. Seek comparison. What do other books of the Bible add to your understanding of the message of John? (This includes references to the Gospel of John found in the epistles.) Using cross-references, a concordance, and other translations, look for further insight from other parts of Scripture as to the message of John.

4. Survey/consult secondary sources. What do commentaries or other Bible study resources say about the purpose of the Gospel of John? Write several key statements you discover in other writings that help you understand John's message. Include references notes.

5. State your conclusions. In light of your findings above, revise your initial proposal. This should form a concise interpretation of the Gospel of John.

Narratives—True Stories about God and His People?

Applying Narratives

Let's look now for ways to summarize discoveries in narrative literature and formulate principles that apply to life. As you study a book of Scripture, take time to look for applications along the way. Keep in mind the four major application suggestions as you work on applying a book of Scripture to your life:

1. Know yourself. What are your particular areas of need and weakness?

2. Relate the book to life. In light of the new relationships (refer to the list on p. 75) you wish to foster in your life, what specific application principles surfaced as you studied John's Gospel? You could probably write dozens of applications from your study of a book. Try to write applications that arise from the principal events and characters there.

Example: 1 Samuel

From David's encounter with Goliath, I learned a valuable lesson about imitating others. Just because other Christians do not have enough faith to meet a certain challenge, that doesn't give me reason to doubt God—if I'm convinced He wants me to act. It may be that God wants to use me in this situation to help others have more faith.

---

3. Meditate on the results. It's a good idea to zero in on one key verse—even in a book study. Once you've chosen that verse, think constantly about what it says and ask God to make it a part of your life.

4. Practice your findings. Throughout your day or week, you can always be consciously applying one principle you have learned from your study. Write a specific action you can take.

Example: 1 Samuel

Using the same truth about David and Goliath as mentioned above, I apply it to a specific situation faced at church. The people at church have been afraid to start an evangelistic Bible study to reach the neighborhood around our church. Instead of criticizing them for their lack of faith, I will take the lead by stepping out in faith and asking them to start a study with me. I am willing to take this action, even if it means standing alone at first.

Observe Interpret Apply

Now you will have an opportunity to apply what you've learned from the Gospel of John to your life.

YOUR TURN

Write five application principles you find in the Gospel of John. Make them personal—affecting your life. (Approximate time: 30 minutes)

Five application principles:

Choose one of these principles and determine what action you can take this week to apply it to your life. Be specific.

CHAPTER 13
Epistles—Letters with a Purpose

Based on the principles of Bible study you have learned in the previous chapters, how might you respond to the following interpretations of passages from Philippians and Colossians?

> The Bible tells us to "Rejoice in the Lord always," which means that, as Christians, we should never feel sad.
>
> —OR—
>
> When Paul warns us not to be taken "captive through hollow and deceptive philosophies," what he is saying is that Christians should only read Christian writers; everything else is a waste of time and will lead us away from true faith.

From your work in Part One, you already may be wondering to yourself: What is the background (the historical context) of these verses, and what do the verses before and after them (the literary context) have to say? You might also ask: What does it mean to rejoice? Is it possible to rejoice and be sad at the same time? How is "rejoicing in the Lord" different from feeling happy? Regarding Paul's warning about deceptive philosophy: In view of the context, what particular philosophies was Paul worried about? How were they different from Christianity? What did Paul propose as a defense against them? With these types of questions at stake, all you have practiced in order to faithfully observe, interpret, and apply Scripture are especially important when studying the epistles.

Observe Interpret Apply

The type of literature called *epistles* makes up all of the New Testament except the Gospels, Acts, and Revelation:

Romans	1 and 2 Timothy
1 and 2 Corinthians	Titus
Galatians	Philemon
Ephesians	Hebrews
Philippians	James
Colossians	1 and 2 Peter
1 and 2 Thessalonians	1, 2, and 3 John
	Jude

The word *epistle* comes from the Greek word *epistolé* meaning "letter or dispatch to a person, or persons." Most of the New Testament epistles were written by the apostles of Jesus after His resurrection and ascension and after the Holy Spirit ushered in the era of the New Testament church. Because they speak about our conduct as members of Christ's Church these letters are often the focus of our affections, study, understanding, and application.

The Nature of Epistles
Epistles were written as ordinary correspondence to first-century Christians. They address specific concerns and needs (typically some doctrinal error or practical behavior) requiring immediate attention. That is why epistles are known as "occasional" documents—they were written for a specific occasion or reason, in response to letters or as the result of information otherwise obtained. They are unique letters in that the Holy Spirit inspired them to be written. God worked through the apostles to pen letters that would not only guide first-century believers in the faith but us as well. Little did those apostles know that 2,000 years later we would still be reading their mail!

Whereas the Gospels present the record of Christ's incarnation (God become human), and Acts preaches Christ's resurrection and the salvation offered in His name, the epistles instruct us in our new life in Christ—how to live out this salvation to the fullest. They interpret the person of Jesus Christ to His church.

The epistles outline the Christian faith. By the time they were completed all major doctrines were in place—each letter emphasizing various subjects. Some studied the nature of Christ; others described God's plan to redeem people who are by nature sinful. Some focused on Christ's return and other events surrounding "end times"; others set out the mechanics of putting a church together in the here and now. And some epistles were just personal notes about a current situation like a run-away slave, or a thanks for hospitality. Whatever the main subject, the epistles are full of God's design for Christian faith and practice.

Epistles — Letters with a Purpose

DIVISIONS AND DISTINCTIVES OF THE EPISTLES

Division — Distinctive (purpose)

ESCHATOLOGICAL
1 Thessalonians
2 Thessalonians

Focus on the doctrine of the return of Christ.

SOTERIOLOGICAL
Romans
1 Corinthians
2 Corinthians
Galatians

Focus on the doctrine of salvation in Christ.

CHRISTOLOGICAL
Ephesians
Philippians
Colossians

Focus on the person of Jesus Christ.

ECCLESIOLOGICAL
1 Timothy
2 Timothy
Titus

Focus on the doctrine and organization of the church.

JEWISH-CHRISTIAN
Hebrews
James

Focus on the special needs of converted Jews of the Dispersion.

GENERAL
1 Peter
2 Peter
1 John
Jude

General truths, written for a broader readership.

PERSONAL
Philemon
2 John
3 John

Written to specific individuals.

The epistles are the earliest form of Christian literature and were probably written and passed along in the following manner:

> The New Testament letters were . . . written on sheets of papyrus with a reed pen and ink, then rolled or folded, tied, and often sealed for privacy and authentication (2 Kings 21:17; Esther 3:12; 8:8; Daniel 12:4; Revelation 5:9). Such letters were sometimes written on waxed tablets with a stylus, mainly for economy since they could be erased. As the official Roman postal service (cursus publicus) was not open to private correspondence, the Christians employed members of the churches as carriers (Acts 15:22; 2 Corinthians 8:16-24; Philippians 2:25; Colossians 4:7-8). While the New Testament letters were written under divine guidance, as well as in human wisdom, in response to specific needs of individuals of churches (1 Corinthians 7:1), it may be questioned whether the authors were ever aware that they were writing for all time and Christendom (2 Timothy 3:16).[1]

The epistles are unique in their organization, having a standard form (in much the same way that our letters follow a common format of date, greeting, main body, close, and signature). Typically (though Hebrews and 1 John lack some of these formal elements), an epistle can be broken down into six parts:

- ☐ Name of the writer (Example: Paul)
- ☐ Name of the recipient (Example: the saints in Christ Jesus at Philippi)
- ☐ Greeting (Example: Grace and peace to you)
- ☐ Prayer or thanksgiving (Example: "I thank my God every time . . .")
- ☐ Body of letter
- ☐ Final greetings and farewell (Example: "The grace of the Lord Jesus Christ be with your spirit")

Speaking of this uniqueness in the epistles, Leland Ryken, in his book *The Literature of the Bible,* says:

> In general, the New Testament epistles do not conform closely to any existing models. For one thing, they show an unusual mixture of the personal letter and the more formalized literary epistle. They contain the personal notes, salutations, and news that informal letters contain, and they are addressed, for the most part, to specific readers. But along with this informality, there is much that is obviously formalized in the epistles.
>
> Their tone is more public than intimate. The personality of the writers is much less important than the religious content of their letters. The writers, indeed, do not write primarily as individual persons but in their role as apostles—as the conveyors of divine truth in a manner reminiscent of the Hebrew prophets.[2]

Epistles—Letters with a Purpose

Categories of Epistles

Biblical scholars have categorized the epistles in several ways. The chart below organizes the epistles according to their nature, author, source, and destination. The chart on page 109 illustrates their distinctives by thinking in theological terms.

Title	Author	Source	Destination
1 Thessalonians	Paul	Corinth	Church at Thessalonica
2 Thessalonians	Paul	Corinth	Church at Thessalonica
1 Corinthians	Paul	Ephesus	Corinthian Christians
Galatians	Paul	Antioch, Ephesus, or Corinth	Christian groups in Central Asia Minor
2 Corinthians	Paul	Ephesus, Macedonia	Corinthian Christians
Romans	Paul	Corinth	Roman church
Philippians	Paul	Rome	Christians at Philippi
Philemon	Paul	Rome	Philemon
Colossians	Paul	Rome	Colossian Christians
Ephesians	Paul	Rome	Church at Ephesus
Pastoral Epistles			
1 Timothy	Paul	Uncertain	Timothy
2 Timothy	Paul	Rome	Timothy
Titus	Paul	Uncertain	Titus
Catholic or General Epistles Destined for Wide Reading			
James	James, half brother of Jesus	Uncertain	Christians of Dispersion
1 Peter	Peter	Uncertain	Christians of Dispersion
2 Peter	Peter	Uncertain	Christians of Dispersion
Jude	Jude, half brother of Jesus	Uncertain	Christians of Dispersion
1 John	John	? Ephesus	Early Christians, Asia Minor
Hebrews	Unknown Christian teacher	Uncertain	Jewish Christians
Asiatic Epistles			
1 John	John		Christians of Dispersion
2 John	John	? Ephesus	"Elect lady"
3 John	John	? Ephesus	Gaius

Taken from the book, *The Zondervan Pictorial Encyclopedia of the Bible* by Merrill C. Tenney. Copyright © 1975, 1976, by the Zondervan Corporation. Used by permission of Zondervan Publishing House.

Observing Epistles

Because of the "letter" nature of epistles, it is particularly important to understand the *occasion* for the writing and the recipients' situation in order to properly interpret and apply epistles. Unlike most other books of the Bible that were written to meet universal needs of a general audience, the epistles were written to specific groups of believers with very direct instructions for application. At the observation stage, we will make a tentative reconstruction of the historical context, including questions such as: What prompted Paul to write to the Philippian church? What was Paul's relationship to the people there?

Observing the Whole

1. Read the book carefully. Get the broad scope of the book by reading it several times. Since most epistles are quite short, you can easily read them through in one sitting.

2. Record your initial impressions. Take time to reflect on and record your initial impressions. At first glance, what do you read and find in answer to the questions of:

Who? (the major characters)
What? (the major events and themes)
Where? (the major locations)
When? (the major divisions of time)

3. Research the setting. This is the point at which you begin to discover the occasion of the epistle. The following elements—all of which deal with the recipients' need and the author's message—will surface as you research the four observation questions.

Who? Who are the main characters? What can you learn about the author? To whom is the book addressed? What do you know, and what more can you learn about the recipients?

Look in:
 ☐ The epistle itself
 ☐ A concordance (note other mentions of these recipients)
 ☐ The Book of Acts (tells us about many of the churches)
 ☐ The Book of Revelation (chapter 2 describes some of the epistolary churches decades later, but with some relevance)

What? What are the key events or ideas in this book? What problems or issues does the epistle address? What is the major teaching or teachings? How would you describe the significance of the content of this particular epistle as compared with the others? What tone is communicated in this letter?

Look in:
 ☐ The epistle itself

Where? Where was the action of this letter taking place? What can you learn about the physical and geographical setting and location that help you understand the book? Locate the church or churches on a map. Where was the author when he was writing this letter?

Epistles—Letters with a Purpose

Look in:
- ☐ The epistle itself
- ☐ The Book of Acts
- ☐ A Bible atlas

When? When did the events of the book take place? What was happening in the life of the author and the recipients at the time the letter was being written? When in the life of the church did the action occur?

Look in:
- ☐ The epistle itself
- ☐ The Book of Acts

New Testament Epistles at a Glance

The chart below pinpoints the historical settings of the New Testament epistles according to the estimated year of composition and their relationship to the Book of Acts.

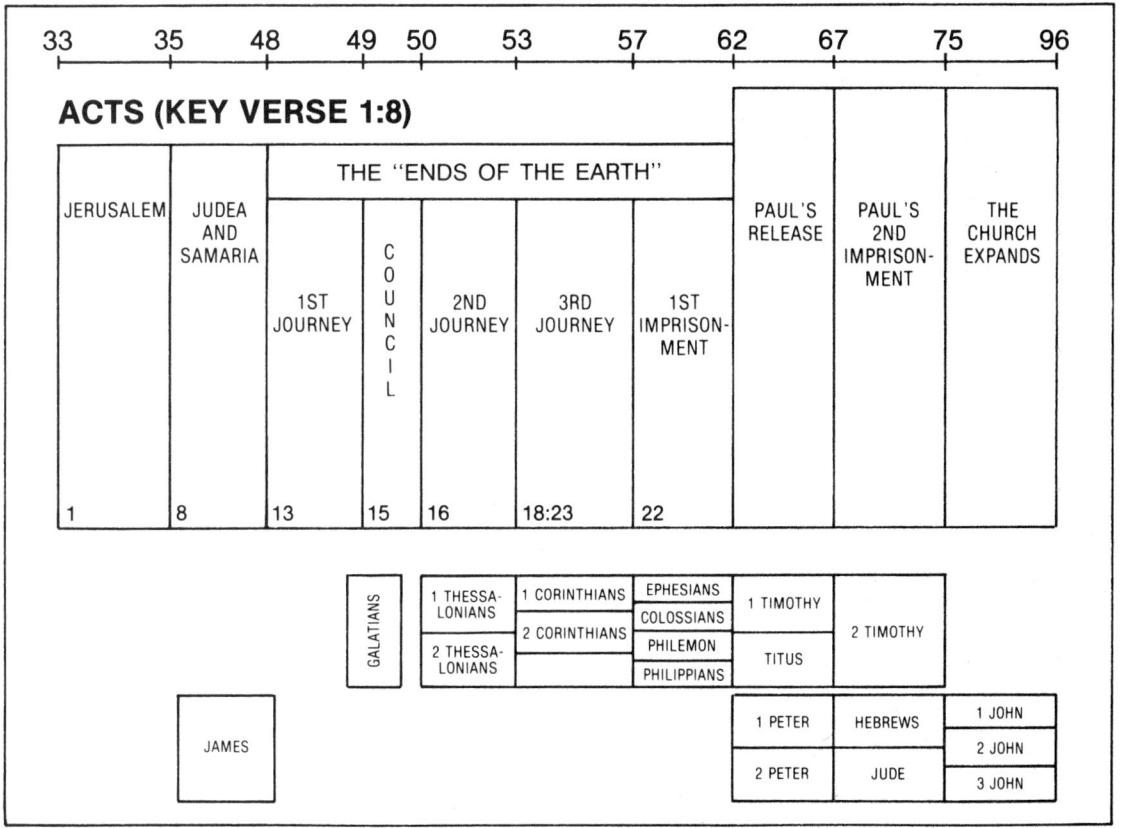

Observe Interpret Apply

The following sample study illustrates how you might observe the Book of Philippians. Look it over carefully. You will then have an opportunity to practice observation in Paul's first letter to the Thessalonians.

Example: Philippians

Who? (the setting)

The Writer: Paul

His circumstances at the time of writing:

1:1	With Timothy as he writes
1:7-9	Has the Philippians on his heart
1:12ff.	Advancing the Gospel while in prison, the whole palace guard is hearing the Gospel
1:17	Many are opposed to his work
1:18	His passion is to preach Christ
2:1-2, 16	Is concerned about the Philippians' unity and maturity
1:30; 2:17	Experiencing great struggles
2:19-23	Eager for news from Philippi, and will send Timothy soon to find out
2:24	Expecting to go to Philippi soon
2:25	Sending Epaphroditus with this letter back to them
3:7-14	Still growing in spite of his own struggles
3:18	Many enemies are opposing him
4:10, 14-18	While in prison, he receives a love gift from the Philippians by way of Epaphroditus. Thanking them
4:21-22	Other Christian brothers with him besides Timothy

His attitude in those circumstances:

1:12	Positive in his outlook
1.18-19	Rejoicing in the Gospel's progress
1:22-26	Selflessness
2:2	Joy—a word that occurs sixteen times in Philippians
2:17-18	Rejoicing in spite of suffering
3:7-14	Pressing on toward maturity
4:4-9	Peace about everything
4:10	Rejoicing over their concern for him
4:11-13	Content in everything

Epistles—Letters with a Purpose

Summary of the author and his circumstances:

Paul's letter to the Philippians is a thank-you letter. Epaphroditus had come to Paul in Rome with a gift from the Philippian church (we don't know if it was money or material goods). Along with his thanks (chapter 4), he reports on his work and encourages the believers as persecution increases in Philippi.

Paul wrote to the Philippians around A.D. 62, while under house arrest in Rome for spreading the teachings of the Gospel throughout the Roman Empire. In spite of his sufferings and restrictions, the Gospel was spreading like wildfire. Paul was probably chained to a guard twenty-four hours a day—but the guards themselves were hearing the Good News and possibly being converted.

The Recipients: The church at Philippi

What we learn about the church from Acts 16:

Paul and Silas founded this group of believers, the first European church

(vv. 9-10)	Paul and Silas were called in a vision to evangelize Macedonia
(v. 12)	Some indication that people were slow to respond to the Gospel
(v. 13)	Looking for a place to pray, they met some women by the river and began sharing the Gospel with them
(vv. 14-15)	First European converts—Lydia and her household
(vv. 16-24)	Paul and Silas falsely accused, arrested, beaten, and jailed for causing disturbances (cast demon out of slave girl)
(vv. 25-34)	While in prison, Philippian jailer was converted and added to the church
(vv. 33ff.)	Paul and Silas released, and encourage the believers before they leave the city

What we learn about the church from Philippians:

1:1	Letter written to an organized church (they've grown since Acts 16)
1:5	Were "partners" with Paul in the work of the Gospel
1:19	Supported Paul in prayer
1:28-30	Now suffering like they had seen Paul do earlier
2:1-4	Seem to need unity as a group of believers
2:25-30	Had cared much for Paul's needs
3:2ff	Were being bothered by teachers who wanted them to take up the Jewish faith
4:1	Were dear friends to Paul
4:2	Some were arguing among themselves
4:9	Paul's life had been an example for them
4:10-18	Had helped Paul for all the years since he first planted the church there

Observe Interpret Apply

YOUR TURN

Having spent time looking over the sample study of Philippians, observe 1 Thessalonians. Record your initial impressions, looking for the *who, what, where,* and *when* of the book. (Approximate time: 2 hours)

Who?

The author:

The recipients:

What?

Epistles — Letters with a Purpose

Where?

When?

Observing the Parts

When observing the parts of an epistle, use the same type of horizontal chart you learned to make for historical narratives (pp. 92–96).

1. Make an initial chart. Because epistles are often short, you can generally divide your chart by paragraphs and chart it that way. Then you are summarizing the major contents for each chapter.

2. Mark the structure. Once you have filled in your chart with the major contents of the epistle, go back and mark the structure of the book using the principles of structure listed in Appendix C.

3. Summarize your findings. Summarize your findings at this step. Make a second chart which reflects the major divisions and structure of the epistle.

Sample charts for Philippians are provided. They illustrate the process from preliminary to final draft. Look them over carefully before beginning your charts of 1 Thessalonians.

PRELIMINARY WORKING CHART
PHILIPPIANS (NASB)

Observe Interpret Apply

	1			2			3		4				
	INTRO.	Focus on Paul		Focus on Philippians			repetition		IN CHURCH	summary			Conclusion summary
GREETINGS — FROM: PAUL & TIMOTHY TO: SAINTS AT PHILIPPI	I THANK GOD FOR: *PARTICIPATION IN THE GOSPEL! I PRAY: *FOR LOVE TO ABOUND IN REAL KNOWLEDGE & DISCERNMENT	PRISON HAS HELPED THE GOSPEL! TO LIVE IS CHRIST; TO DIE IS GAIN HARD-PRESSED IN BOTH DIRECTIONS I SHALL REMAIN... FOR YOU!	STAND FIRM *DON'T BE ALARMED BY OPPOSITION *YOU ARE SUFFERING FOR CHRIST	BE ENCOURAGED IN CHRIST UNITY HUMILITY THE EXAMPLE OF CHRIST HUMILIATION & EXALTATION	WORK OUT YOUR SALVATION IN FEAR & TREMBLING GOD IS WORKING IN YOU REJOICE	PAUL'S PERSONAL INTEREST IN THEM TIMOTHY— PROVEN SERVANT EPAPHRODITUS —CLOSE TO DEAD FOR CHRIST	BEWARE DOGS EVIL DOERS FALSE CIRCUMCISION PAUL'S TESTIMONY: JEW OF JEWS ALL LOSS TO KNOW CHRIST PRESS ON TO MATURITY	FOLLOW US BEWARE OF ENEMIES OF THE CROSS: THEY ARE EARTHLY CONTRAST WE ARE CITIZENS OF HEAVEN	4:1 STAND FIRM EUODIA & SYNTYCHE LIVE IN HARMONY CLEMENT ALSO	REJOICE BE PATIENT PRAY PEACE	THINK ON THINGS ABOVE PRACTICE OUR EXAMPLE	PAUL: CONTENT IN ALL CIRCUMSTANCES PHILIPPIANS HELPED WHEN NO ONE ELSE WOULD THEIR NEEDS WILL BE MET	GREETINGS	CLOSING WORDS—GRACE
1:1-2	3-11	12-26	27-30	2:1-11	12-18	19-30	3:1-16	17-21	4:1-3	4-7	8-9	10-20	21-22	23

IN WORLD → → IN CHURCH

Note interchange between Paul's life and theirs

→ Repetition of idea of persecution
  - explanation
  - illustration
  - their conduct in the world
  - 1st pivot — moves to personal personal matters
  - Paul's personal concern
  - illustration / example
  - Paul's maturity
  - The maturity of the Philippians
  - their concern for Paul

Recurring themes:
* stand firm
* beware
* rejoice and joy
* suffering and persecution

Epistles — Letters with a Purpose

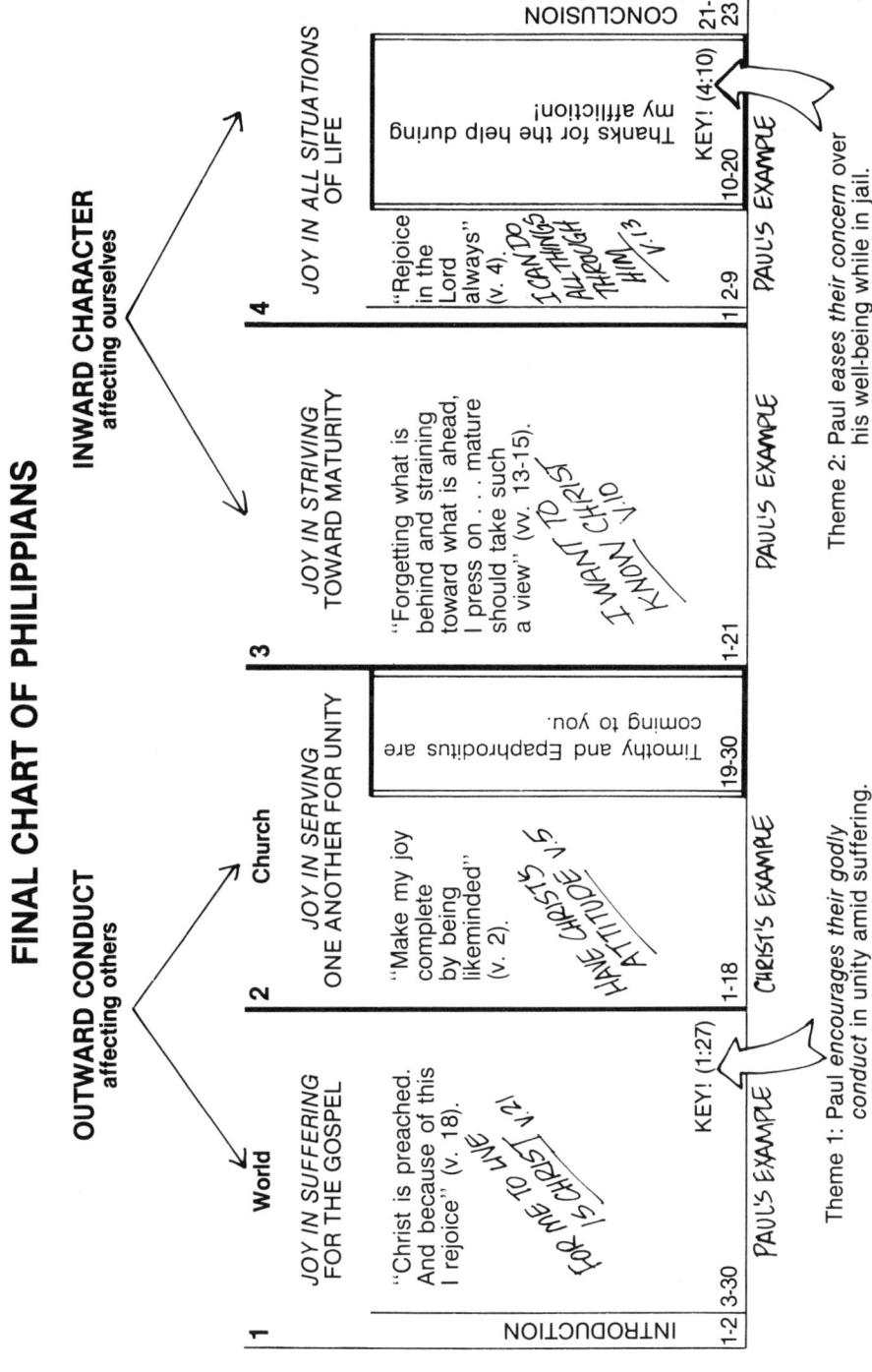

Observe Interpret Apply

YOUR TURN

Having examined the charts for Philippians, make a book chart of your own for 1 Thessalonians. Space is provided for a first draft and a final chart. After you have completed your first draft, go back and mark in the principles of structure from Appendix C that you find in 1 Thessalonians. Then organize your final draft. (Approximate time: 90 minutes)

BOOK CHART OF 1 THESSALONIANS
First Draft

BOOK CHART OF I THESSALONIANS
Final Draft

Interpreting Epistles

Most of our difficulties in understanding the epistles stem from their "occasional" nature, which we discussed earlier. These letters were written to other people, not to us. It may help to think of how you write a letter to someone you know. When referring to an experience you have shared, you don't include the details because you assume the person who receives the letter knows what you're talking about. A similar dynamic is at work in the epistles. Certain questions we might have concerning the historical context, or references made without giving any explanation, we may only be able to answer in part—and we need to content ourselves with that reality. We can be sure, however, that what God wants us to know and obey in these letters He has made clear. (Incidentally, this is a good test when choosing a commentary: How does the scholar treat difficult passages—does he or she try to have an answer for everything or is there a willingness to admit uncertainty where the text itself is not clear? A humble attitude in Bible study is a sign of maturity and integrity—not doubt.)

Context is the key, so *think in terms of paragraphs* (the literary context) when trying to understand what the writer is saying and why he is saying it. This will help guard against the temptation to proof text (use a passage of Scripture to prove a point not in its original context).

Two important questions to ask of every epistle:
    Why did the author write what he did?
    What is the underlying message or theme of his letter?

Recall from chapters 7–8 that these two "purpose" questions are thought of as the *need* and the *message*.

▶ *The need.* Bearing in mind that the epistles were written in response to a specific need in the lives of the recipients, the first task of interpreting an epistle is to relate that need—or the occasion which prompted the author's writing—to the recipients.

▶ *The message.* Here is where you summarize in a sentence or two the solution the author gives to address the needs of his readers. What specific information does he give to address those needs? How does his message contribute to the canon of Scripture? Notice how, in the example on page 123, two key verses have been used to crystallize the two central messages of Philippians. Whenever you can, find a key verse or verses that reflect the overall purpose of the book.

Answers to the interpretation questions of *need* and *message* can be formed by looking in the same four places we always look.

Epistles — Letters with a Purpose

1. State an initial proposal based on the content. Before looking for the answers, write what you think are the need and message of the epistle you are studying. Remember, your proposal should come from reading that book, not someone else's comments on it. You will use secondary sources later.

2. Search the context. In the epistles, the immediate context is the other companion epistles. For instance, 1 and 2 Peter are companion books and are able to shed light on each other. The same applies to Paul's two letters to the Corinthians and the three letters of John. Companions to Philippians would be the other epistles Paul wrote from prison: Ephesians, Colossians, and Philemon.

3. Seek comparison. The Bible itself sheds light on its own meaning. Sound interpretation takes into account the whole of scriptural teaching. Cross-references, other New Testament books, and other translations can add to your understanding of an epistle's meaning.

4. Survey/Consult the secondary sources. When you have completed a thorough study of the biblical material, see what secondary sources add to your understanding. They often provide insight from wise and godly people. Secondary sources include commentaries, atlases, Bible dictionaries, theology books, and other reference books about the Bible.

5. State your conclusions. Having consulted the necessary resources to help you interpret your book, restate your initial proposal in light of any new insights.

Example: Philippians

▶ *The Need:* The Christians at Philippi were suffering greatly for the sake of the Gospel and needed the example of Paul's suffering to give them courage. They were also concerned over Paul's well-being, which is a second need addressed by the letter.

▶ *The Message:* Paul, from his jail cell in Rome, penned this letter to the Philippians to encourage their godly conduct in the midst of suffering. "Whatever happens," Paul wrote, "conduct yourselves in a manner worthy of the Gospel of Christ" (1:27).

Paul also wrote to ease their concern over his well-being: "I rejoice greatly in the Lord that at last you have renewed your concern for me" (4:10).

Observe Interpret Apply

YOUR TURN

You probably already have a good idea of what 1 Thessalonians is all about, since you have already spent several hours studying it. Now make an initial proposal as to the purpose of this epistle. Then go through the steps for finding the answers for interpretation.

The Purpose of 1 Thessalonians
1. Initial Proposal—Study the content. Give your initial responses to these two questions. Write one or two sentences for each.

▶ *The Reader's Need:*

▶ *The Author's Message:*

2. Search the context and seek comparison. What do other books of the Bible add to your understanding of the message of 1 Thessalonians?

3. Survey/consult the secondary sources. What do commentaries or other Bible study tools say about the purpose of 1 Thessalonians? Write several key statements you discovered from other writings that helped you better understand this book.

4. State your conclusions. In light of your findings, how would you revise your initial proposal.

▶ *The Reader's Need:*

▶ *The Author's Message:*

Applying Epistles

In applying the epistles to our lives, look for principles of truth that are meant to affect our behavior and attitude toward God and others. Your applications should arise naturally out of the principles you discovered during the observation and interpretation phases of your study.

General Principles for Applying the Epistles

1. Try to distinguish between what is cultural, and therefore belongs only to the first century, and what transcends culture, and therefore applies to all people everywhere. For example, Paul instructs Timothy to bring him his cloak from Troas (2 Timothy 4:13), but common sense tells us that this instruction does not apply to us today.

Although this example seems obvious, there are passages in the epistles that are less so. The challenge to us is to be consistent in applying our methods and let the Word of God challenge those areas in our lives where our culture, or religious tradition, or personal experience is determining how we interpret Scripture.

2. A passage cannot mean now what it never meant to the original audience. This is why the first step of inductive Bible study is observation, which asks: What was happening at that time?

3. Where we share comparable life situations with those of the first century, God's Word to us is the same as it was to the original audience. Again, careful investigation of the original situation in observation and interpretation is crucial for the stage of application.

While this principle does not specifically answer a question you may have, it does provide some limits as to what are possible acceptable answers. For example, in 1 Corinthians 8–10, Paul addresses the issue of food sacrificed to idols. It is unlikely that we will ever be in a situation where we will face this same concern that confronted the believers of the first century.[3]

Here are four suggestions for applying Scripture:

1. Know yourself. What are your personal strengths and weaknesses, and how does Scripture speak to your areas of need? (Review our notes on page 73 and make additional comments at this point.)

2. Relate the epistle to life. What application principles come to mind as you think of 1 Thessalonians in light of the series of new relationships (p. 75)?

> **Example: Philippians 4:19**
>
> In the last chapter of Philippians, Paul writes what has become a favorite verse for many Christians. We, however, often fail to see both sides of the principle.
>
> *Principle 1:* As I do what I can to meet the needs of people around me, (as the Philippians met Paul's needs), I can trust God to meet my needs (as Paul assured the Philippians He would).
>
> *Principle 2:* From Paul's letter to the Philippians, I learn a lot about how God supplies all my needs, not all my wants.

3. Meditate on the results. You can carry the fruit of your Bible study with you throughout the day by zeroing in on one key verse, and meditating on it.

4. Practice your findings. Ask yourself, "How can I put this truth to work in my life?" Then write one or two specific actions you can take to "put feet" to what you've learned.

YOUR TURN

Write five application principles you find in the Book of 1 Thessalonians. Try to make them personal. (Approximate time: 30 minutes)

Five application principles:

What one action will you take this week to apply one of these principles in your life? Be specific.

CHAPTER 14
Wisdom Literature and Poetry—Truths to Remember

The Book of Psalms is a handbook for prayer. I sometimes read the psalms aloud as prayers to God; they seem to express in such a rich way what I'm feeling, whether it's joy or sorrow, hope or discouragement, trust or doubt. Many believers read through one chapter of Proverbs or several psalms each day as a matter of habit.

The wisdom literature and poetry of Scripture include:

Wisdom Literature
Job
Proverbs
Ecclesiastes

Poetic Literature
Psalms
Song of Solomon

These five books overflow with personal and practical spiritual truths waiting to be discovered through diligent study.

Why study the wisdom and poetry books of the Bible at the same time? There are several reasons. Because of their similarity, these books were arranged in one central location in the Old Testament. And, with the exception of Job (the first book of the Bible ever written), they were all written at about the same time—during Israel's zenith under David and Solomon's leadership. A nation often produces its best literature during times of great victory and prosperity, and this was certainly true of Israel. Thus the God-given understanding and wisdom of Israel's two greatest kings was divinely preserved in the forms of psalms and proverbs.

Because of the similarities between wisdom literature and poetic literature, the opportunities to practice studying this literature will focus on the book of Job. The unique poetry of Psalms and the Song of Solomon will be noted at the end of this chapter.

Characteristics of Wisdom Literature

Wisdom has been defined as "the discipline of applying truth to one's life in the light of experience."[1] Three characteristics distinguish this type of literature.

1. Advice being given is from a wise man. In wisdom literature, the narrator is a wise person who has learned a great deal about human experience. He gives advice on this experience in the form of declarations. In Hebrew culture, three types of leaders influenced the people's behavior and taught them how to relate to God: prophets, priests, and wise men. Job, Proverbs, and Ecclesiastes are collections of the sayings of those wise men of Israel.

2. Extensive use of proverbs. A proverb is "a brief, popular epigram or maxim." It is a general truth, recognized by all, stated concisely (like "a rolling stone gathers no moss"). Proverbs tend to use figurative language and express things suggestively rather than in detail.

3. General truths stated in short literary units. Wisdom literature uses a variety of literary devices other than the proverbs to teach general truths. These devices include:

> **Parallelism:** the use of two statements side by side to present a general truth in different ways. There are two kinds of common parallelism:
>
> *Antithetical Parallelism:* the second statement expresses the antithesis or opposite of the first statement.
>
> Example from Proverbs 12:1
>
> > *Whoever loves discipline loves knowledge,*
> > *but he who hates correction is stupid.*

Synonymous Parallelism: the second statement repeats the sense of the first statement in slightly different words.

Example from Proverbs 12:14

> *From the fruit of his lips a man is filled with good things*
> *as surely as the work of his*
> *hands rewards him.*

(We will come back to parallelism in other forms when we study the poetic books.)

Comparison: the association of like things.

Example from Proverbs 12:9

> *Better to be a nobody and yet have a servant*
> *than pretend to be somebody and have no food.*

Metaphors and Similes: using figurative language to compare one object or idea with another.

Example from Proverbs 12:4

> *A wife of noble character is her husband's crown,*
> *but a disgraceful wife is like decay in*
> *his bones.*

Portraits: extended pictures that represent a type of person.

Example: Proverbs 31:10-31 is the portrait of a wise and mature woman of God.

Brief Narrative: a brief description of an event or experience.

Example: In Ecclesiastes, Solomon includes several brief descriptions of his search for the meaning of life (Ecclesiastes 2:4-11). Proverbs 7:6-23 depicts in narrative form a prostitute's enticement of a young man who lacked judgment.

Wisdom Literature and Poetry—Truths to Remember

Vignette: a short descriptive sketch or scene; a mini-picture.

Example: The wise work of a diligent farmer is pictured in Proverbs 27:23-27.

The use of literary devices like these makes wisdom books unique. You will have an opportunity to get better acquainted with the wisdom books when you begin observation work in the Book of Job.

Observing Wisdom Literature

We often misunderstand or misapply the wisdom writings of the Bible, and thereby lose the benefits God intended us to receive from them.

> When properly understood and used, wisdom [literature] is a helpful resource for Christian living. When misused, it can provide a basis for selfish, materialistic, short-sighted behavior—just the opposite of what God intended.[2]

The first wisdom book we will look at is Job. You might wonder at first why Job is included in the category of wisdom literature—so much of the "wisdom" expressed in the book seems humanistic and void of seeing life from God's point of view. The key to understanding this book, however, is to differentiate between the wisdom of Job and that of his well-meaning "friends"—Bildad, Zophar, Eliphaz, and Elihu—who offered Job all kinds of wrong advice and incorrect conclusions. The wisdom taught in Job might best be called "true wisdom." Fee and Stuart comment:

> As you read through the book you will notice that it takes the form of a highly structured conversation or dialogue. This dialogue has a very important goal: to establish convincingly in the mind of the reader that what happens in life does not always happen because God desires it or because it is fair. . . .
>   This is true wisdom at its finest. The reader of the Book of Job learns what is simply the world's wisdom, seemingly logical but actually wrong, and what constitutes God's wisdom and what builds confidence in God's sovereignty and righteousness. Thus the dialogue and the story line combine to make it the Old Testament's paramount exemplar of speculative wisdom.[3]

In contrast, the Book of Proverbs might be called a book of "practical wisdom," since it teaches the *ways* of wisdom. In it we find one of the greatest concentrations of good advice parents could ever hope to give their children. This collection of "words from the wise" says that in the normal course of events, abundant spiritual life comes to those who consistently follow its teachings. One caution about the Book of Proverbs: those wise sayings are statements of what normally happens in the routine of human events. They are not intended as promises. Thus, when we train a child "in the way he should go" as Proverbs 22:6 instructs, we should understand that most (but not all) children will stay in these paths. Even so, Proverbs offers great advice.

My son, if you accept my words
    and store up my commands within you,
turning your ear to wisdom
    and applying your heart to understanding,
and if you call out for insight
    and cry aloud for understanding,
and if you look for it as for silver
    and search for it as for hidden treasure,
then you will understand the fear of the LORD
    and find the knowledge of God.
For the LORD gives wisdom,
    and from His mouth come knowledge and understanding.
He holds victory in store for the upright,
    He is a shield to those whose walk is blameless,
for He guards the course of the just
    and protects the way of His faithful ones.
    —*Proverbs 2:1-8*

Unlike Proverbs, Ecclesiastes is more like Job. Ecclesiastes often puzzles its readers and is frequently misunderstood. Its message of cynicism and ultimate meaninglessness could leave us wondering whether this book even belongs in the Bible! Actually, Ecclesiastes is a storehouse of wisdom about the meaning of life. Its "cynical wisdom" fits into the category of wisdom literature for several reasons: It is written by a wise man, Solomon; it contains declarations of wisdom concerning human experience; and it contains proverbs, brief narratives, and simple portraits.

Not only was the Teacher wise, but also he imparted knowledge to the people. He pondered and searched out and set in order many proverbs.
    —*Ecclesiastes 12:9*

Leland Ryken explains why Ecclesiastes has been so misunderstood, and how to avoid making the same mistake.

Ecclesiastes might well be the most misunderstood book in the Bible. Most commentators have found the theme of the book to be inconsistent with the rest of biblical teaching. How such a view of the book arose is baffling. It is no exaggeration to say that this book espouses the most basic theme of biblical literature—that life lived by purely earthly or human values, without faith in God and supernatural values, is meaningless and futile. The key term in the book is the phrase "under the sun." This phrase, or its equivalent "under the heaven" occurs thirty times in the book and denotes that which is only earthly. To be "under the sun" is to be earth-bound, cut off from the supernatural order.

    In developing his theme, the writer has chosen a common literary device. He demonstrates at length the inadequacy of any world view other than a theocentric one, and he combines with this demonstration an affirmation of an alternate worldview. This means that the individual passages must be placed carefully in their contexts. If we read every passage as being equally indicative of the writer's settled contradictory statements, we are left with a meaningless collection of contradictory statements, for it is indisputable that the views of some passages contradict those of others. Actually, the contradiction is partly understood to be the conclusions that emerge when he limits his gaze to the earthly scene. When the narrator voices despair over the futility of life under the sun, he is not affirming this as his final answer to life's existence.[4]

Observing the Whole

1. Read the book carefully. When beginning your study of wisdom literature, skim through the book in one sitting. Because of the length of these books, read at a little slower pace, looking for major themes or topics. [Hint: There are no major characters to deal with in Proverbs, except those discussed abstractly: the harlot or the sluggard. In Ecclesiastes, notice especially the two different perspectives Solomon has on life: sometimes all is vanity; at other times, life has rich meaning. What makes the difference?]

2. Record your initial impressions. As you read, note your initial observations. Get a general overview of the book's contents, including the major characters, events, and themes. [Hint: Location (where) and timing (when) are not major considerations in Proverbs because it is a book of timeless principles. And in Ecclesiastes, the major content of the book revolves around the *what* question.] At this stage, only record the broad facts about:

Who? (the major characters)
What? (the major events and themes)
Where? (the major locations)
When? (the major divisions of time)

Observing the Parts

To understand the parts is to grasp the whole of the book. Recall from the previous chapters that this is accomplished by making a chart of the book. In your study of wisdom literature, you follow the same guidelines for chart making that you learned in chapter 12:

1. Make a first draft book chart.
2. Mark the principles of structure (refer to Appendix C).
3. Revise your chart.

Now it's time for you to practice what you've learned on the Book of Job.

Observe Interpret Apply

YOUR TURN

There are two parts to this observation exercise: (1) record your impressions of the Book of Job as a whole, and (2) chart its structure and define its parts. If you need more detailed instructions concerning book charting, refer to chapter 12.

Observing the whole: Record your initial impressions of the book of Job, answering the questions *who, what, where,* and *when.* (Approximate time: 2 hours)

Who? (the author)

Who? (the characters)

What?

Wisdom Literature and Poetry—Truths to Remember

Where?

When?

Observing the parts: On the following page make an observation chart for the Book of Job. After making a first draft, mark it with the principles of structure (refer to Appendix C). Then draw a revised chart.

Observe Interpret Apply

BOOK CHART OF JOB
First draft

BOOK CHART OF JOB
Final draft

Observe Interpret Apply

Interpreting Wisdom Literature

When interpreting a book as a whole unit, our primary concern is to discover the purpose of the book: the readers' *need* and the author's *message*. In *The Literature and Meaning of Scripture,* Morris A. Inch and C. Hassell Bullock explain,

> To interpret wisdom literature, one must understand the cultural situations in which it arose. Probably the two key areas were the royal court and the teacher-pupil relationship. From the Old Testament it is clear that wise men, as well as astrologers and soothsayers, flourished in the courts of Egypt and Babylon. Moses encountered them in Egypt (Exodus 7:11) and Daniel became the leader of Nebuchadnezzar's core of wise men because of his ability to interpret dreams (Daniel 2:48). These men were called on to give advice in matters of state, particularly in relation to military campaigns and strategy. The lives of Nebuchadnezzar's wise men were in jeopardy when they could not meet his demands (Daniel 2:12). In Israel, Ahithophel was a gifted counselor whose wisdom was highly regarded by both David and Absalom (2 Samuel 16:23).
>
> Solomon was renowned as the wisest man in Israel, and God gave him a wisdom that surpassed that of the Egyptians and the men of the East (1 Kings 4:30). During his reign, interest in wisdom literature reached its peak, and Solomon himself was acknowledged as the author of 3,000 proverbs (1 Kings 4:32) and the Books of Proverbs, Ecclesiastes, and the Song of Solomon.
>
> Wisdom also developed within the broader framework of education. The "wise man" (or woman) was generally an older person who instructed the young about life. Often in Proverbs "my son" may refer to the pupil who was under the tutelage of a wise man. Their relationship was like that of a father and son.[5]

According to Jewish tradition, the fathers were responsible for training their offspring in the ways of wisdom. Even though we live in a different culture and a different era, today's Christian dads long to pass on their faith in similar ways. Here is how Moses instructed fathers to teach their children all of the principles of the Law:

> *Hear, O Israel: The LORD our God, the LORD is one. Love the LORD your God with all your heart and with all your soul and with all your strength. These commandments that I give you today are to be upon your hearts. Impress them on your children. Talk about them when you sit at home and when you walk along the road, when you lie down and when you get up. Tie them as symbols on your hands and bind them on your foreheads. Write them on the doorframes of your houses and on your gates.*
>
> —*Deuteronomy 6:4-9*

1. State an initial proposal based on the content. Your interpretation should arise first out of the book you are studying—not out of someone else's comments on what the book means. Try to state what you think is the *need* and *message* of the book in one or two sentences each.

Wisdom Literature and Poetry—Truths to Remember

> **Example: Ecclesiastes**
>
> ▶ *The Need:* Some people feel that no matter what they do, all of life is meaningless.
>
> ▶ *The Message:* We can accept the limitations of our universe, acknowledge God's authority by obeying His commands, and thereby enjoy life as it is.

2. Search the context. In the case of wisdom and poetic literature, the context is the period of history during which the book was written.

3. Seek comparison. See what cross-references and different Bible translations add to your understanding of the book you are studying.

4. Survey/consult the secondary sources. Only after you've done a thorough study of your primary source—the Bible—should you consult secondary sources. Commentaries and Bible dictionaries are especially helpful resources for wisdom literature and poetry studies.

5. State your conclusions. Restate your initial proposal in light of your added insight.

YOUR TURN

By now you probably have a good feel for the contents of the Book of Job. Make an initial proposal as to the purpose of this wisdom book. Then go through the other steps for finding the answers for interpretation, filling in the spaces that follow. (Approximate time: 2 hours)

Observe Interpret Apply

1. Initial proposal—Study the content. Give your initial responses to these two questions, each in one or two sentences.

▶ *The Reader's Need:*

▶ *The Author's Message:*

2. Search the context. What do other books of the Bible add to your understanding of the message of Job?

3. Survey/consult the secondary sources. Note several key statements you discovered from commentaries or other study tools that helped you better understand Job better.

4. State your conclusions. In light of your findings, how would you revise your initial proposal. Restate your interpretive statements below.

▶ *The Reader's Need:*

▶ *The Author's Message:*

Applying Wisdom Literature
Use the same four principles of application learned in chapters 9 and 10 to guide application of wisdom literature.

1. Know yourself. What sections or statements from the book seem especially applicable to your current situation in life?

2. Relate the book to life. In light of the series of new relationships (p. 75), what specific application principles come to mind?

3. Meditate on the results. Zero in on one key verse. Think about what it says during the day and ask God to make it a part of your life.

4. Practice your findings. Ask yourself, "How should I respond based on what I've learned?"

Observe Interpret Apply

YOUR TURN

Make notes below about ways that you could apply the Book of Job. (Approximate time: 60 minutes)

What sections or statements from Job seem especially applicable to your current situation?

Review the series of relationships on page 75. Which of these grow naturally out of Job's words or experience?

Wisdom Literature and Poetry—Truths to Remember

Select one verse or paragraph from the Book of Job that you think summarizes the message of the entire book. Write it here. Spend time meditating on that text. Rephrase it as a prayer. Ask God to show you ways to make it live in your inner being and in your actions.

Write five application principles you find in the Book of Job. Try to make them personal.

What one action can you take this week to apply one of these principles in your life? Be specific.

Special Features of Poetic Literature

The Book of Psalms and the Song of Solomon are unique in that they are filled with the range of human emotion. Whereas much of the Bible tells us what we should *know* about God and our relationship with Him, Psalms tells us how we *feel* about God. In contrast, the Song of Solomon tells us what it feels like to love another human being deeply, passionately. Leland Ryken says:

Observe Interpret Apply

> What is God like? To this question the psalmists give a variety of answers. Their answers must be studied within the framework of lyric poetry rather than systematic theology for the obvious reason that they wrote lyric poems, not theological treatises. They were less concerned to convey information about God than to write about their own experience of God and of their response to Him. Their utterances, moreover, are poetic in form having all the characteristics of lyric poetry and asking to be understood and enjoyed in those terms.[6]

The Song of Solomon and many of the psalms and were actually written as songs. These songs intentionally appeal to our emotions, evoking a heartfelt response. The psalms were the prayer book and hymnal of God's people, and were used in much the same way as our modern hymnals today. They address God or express truth about Him in song. The Song of Solomon expresses the emotions of a man and a woman, set within the context of courtship and marriage.

Hebrew Parallelism

The predominant feature of Hebrew poetry is the repetition of meaning in parallel expressions, so we must study the relationship between the parallel units to determine the meaning of the whole verse.

Hebrew poetry falls into six major categories of parallelism, two of which were described on pages 129–130.

> **1. Synonymous Parallelism:** the closest similarity expressed between each of the two consecutive lines.
>
> > *O LORD, how many are my foes!*
> > *How many rise up against me!*
> > *—Psalm 3:1*
>
> **2. Synthetic Parallelism:** the second line takes up and develops a bit further the thought begun in the first line.
>
> > *For the LORD is the great God,*
> > *the great King above all gods.*
> > *—Psalm 95:3*
>
> **3. Emblematic Parallelism:** the first line expresses an idea and the second line is a metaphorical illumination of the first.
>
> > *As the deer pants for streams of water,*
> > *so my soul pants for You, O God.*
> > *—Psalm 42:1*

Wisdom Literature and Poetry — Truths to Remember

4. Antithetical Parallelism: the parallel elements are set in balance through the use of opposing or contrasting thoughts.

*For the L*ORD *watches over the way of the righteous,*
but the way of the wicked will perish.
—Psalm 1:6

5. Climactic Parallelism: the second line repeats exactly an expression from the first line with the addition or subtraction of an idea.

*Ascribe to the L*ORD, *O mighty ones,*
*ascribe to the L*ORD *glory and strength.*
—Psalm 29:1

6. Formal Parallelism: the second parallel expression simply continues the thought of the first.

I have installed my King
on Zion, my holy hill.
—Psalm 2:6

It is helpful to be able to identify poetic parallelisms when studying the details of a particular psalm. These same categories of parallelism apply to other biblical books where poetry appears.

Classification of the Psalms

Five Books:
>Book 1 (Psalms 1–41)
>Book 2 (Psalms 42–72)
>Book 3 (Psalms 73–89)
>Book 4 (Psalms 90–106)
>Book 5 (Psalms 107–50)

Types of Psalms:
>*Royal Psalms:* 2, 18, 20, 21, 45, 72, 89, 101, 110, 144.
>They anticipate Christ as King.
>
>*Alphabetic Psalms:* 9, 10, 25, 34, 37, 111, 112, 119, 145.
>They employ some arrangement based on the Hebrew alphabet.

Penitential Psalms: 6, 25, 32, 38, 39, 40, 51, 102, 130.
These psalms express deep contrition for sin committed.

Messianic Psalms: 2, 8, 16, 22, 45, 69, 72, 89, 110, 118, 132.
They preview the person and work of the coming Messiah.

Imprecatory Psalms: 52, 58, 59, 68, 109, 140.
Sometimes called the "psalms of hate," these psalms implore God's vindication of His people against their persecutors.

Hallelujah Psalms: 111–13, 115–17, 146–50.
These psalms employ the term *Hallelujah,* meaning "Praise Jah" (Jehovah).

Elohistic Psalms: 42–83.
They often use the name *Elohim* for God. (Others psalms use the name Jehovah.)

Ascent Psalms: 120–134.
They were recited or sung as the pilgrims went up to Jerusalem to celebrate the feasts.[7]

Figurative Language

Some words and pictures in Scripture cannot be taken literally. We broadly classify this type of material as figurative language, and include in this category figures of speech, parables, and symbols.

Scripture is filled with figures of speech. They contribute to the beauty and enduring quality of the Bible. We need to learn to recognize these figures and interpret them carefully. Understanding the cultural and linguistic context is key. For instance, in Psalm 22:16, David compares his enemies to "dogs" which have surrounded him. This may not seem like such a terrible thing to us, since in our culture dogs are generally loving household pets. But in David's culture, dogs were usually wild animals that roamed in packs and viciously attacked anything or anyone who fell prey to them. Here is where a book about Bible cultures and customs can help explain the linguistic context of the passage you are studying.

Figures of Speech:
A list of some of the more important figures of speech found in Scripture follows:

Simile: a comparison of things which are essentially alike, expressed directly through the use of a word of comparison such as *like* or *as*.

Wisdom Literature and Poetry — Truths to Remember

He is like a tree planted by streams of water,
which yields its fruit in season

—*Psalm 1:3*

Metaphor: an implied comparison in which a word or phrase that is ordinarily used to describe one object or idea is applied to another.

"I am the true vine, and My Father is the gardener."

—*John 15:1*

Metonymy: the use of the name of one thing for that of another associated with or suggested by it.

Then they sweep past like the wind and go on—
guilty men, whose own strength is their god.

—*Habakkuk 1:11*

Synecdoche: the use of a part to stand for the whole or the reverse of that.

Abraham replied, "They have Moses and the Prophets; let them listen to them."

—*Luke 16:29*

Hyperbole: an obvious exaggeration, not meant to be taken literally.

Where can we go? Our brothers have made us lose heart. They say, "The people are stronger and taller than we are; the cities are large, with walls up to sky. We even saw the Anakites there."

—*Deuteronomy 1:28*

Irony: a subtly sarcastic expression in which the intended meaning of the words used is the direct opposite of their usual sense.

At noon Elijah began to taunt them. "Shout louder!" he said. "Surely he is a god! Perhaps he is deep in thought, or busy, or traveling. Maybe he is sleeping and must be awakened."

—*1 Kings 18:27*

Personification: the giving of human characteristics to inanimate objects, ideas, or qualities.

The LORD said, "What have you done? Listen! Your brother's blood cries out to Me from the ground."

—*Genesis 4:10*

Rhetorical questions: the asking of questions without expecting answers. The author is thus implying that the answer to the question is so obvious and indisputable that the question needs no reply.

Who will bring any charge against those whom God has chosen? It is God who justifies.
—*Romans 8:33*

Apostrophe: a turning away from the direct subject to address other topics; an exclamatory digression.

I am worn out from groaning;
all night long I flood my bed with weeping
and drench my couch with tears.
My eyes grow weak with sorrow;
they fail because of all my foes.
Away from me, all you who do evil,
for the L<small>ORD</small> *has heard my weeping*
The L<small>ORD</small> *has heard my cry for mercy;*
the L<small>ORD</small> *accepts my prayer.*
All my enemies will be ashamed and dismayed;
they will turn back in sudden disgrace.
—*Psalm 6:6-10*

Interpreting Figures of Speech

1. Be alert to figurative language in Scripture. Knowing the types of figures will make you more sensitive to their occurrence in the Bible.

2. Interpret a figure literally, adhering to the ordinary meaning of a term or expression, unless it absolutely does not make sense. Since language is normally to be understood literally, take a figure of speech at its face value unless it is contrary to the nature of God or the Scriptures.

3. Don't overinterpret similes and metaphors. Be careful not to stretch a figure of speech beyond the meaning the author intended. Remember:
   ☐ Generally, there is one point of comparison.
   ☐ Cultural background can help define the figure of speech itself.
   ☐ Use the theme, context, and plan of the book to find the exact meaning of the figure of speech.

Rules for Interpreting Parables

Jesus used many parables to teach about the kingdom of God. Parable means "to place beside"; a truth is placed beside a story to illuminate and explain it.

Wisdom Literature and Poetry—Truths to Remember

Here are six rules of thumb for interpreting parables:

1. Study the story as a story until you get the full impact of its meaning in that day.

2. Study the story with strict regard to the author's interpretation and application. (He will tell you what it means.)

3. Study with strict regard to the setting of the context and the theme of the passage.

4. List the points of comparison between the truth and the story.

5. Some elements of the story have no meaning. Don't try to tack a meaning onto every element.

6. Find the one central teaching of the parable. Don't get sidetracked in the fine details.

YOUR TURN

Reread the culmination of Job's story in Job 38–42. Find as many different types of parallelism as you can and note them below. See how many figures of speech you can find in these chapters and note them also.

Parallelism in Job 38–42	Figures of Speech in Job 38–42

Parallelism in Job 38–42 (continued)	Figures of Speech in Job 38–42 (continued)

Wisdom Literature and Poetry — Truths to Remember

Why did Job repent?
Write a brief parable to explain your answer.

Alternate activity: Answer the question, "Why did Job repent," as if you were Job explaining your actions to your newly restored friends.

CHAPTER 15
Prophecy and Revelation— Judgment with Hope

The last type of biblical literature we will study is prophetic books. This category includes all of the Old Testament prophets and the New Testament Book of Revelation. The prophets played a major role in the history of God's chosen people and they have many valuable lessons for us today as well.

From the time your forefathers left Egypt until now, day after day, again and again I sent you My servants the prophets.
— Jeremiah 7:25

As you'll see from studying these books, many of God's chosen people refused to listen to the message of the prophets. But, if we will let them, the prophets can speak to us of God's justice, judgment, love, and mercy.

Historically, the prophets have been divided into two categories:

Major Prophets	Minor Prophets	
Isaiah	Hosea	Nahum
Jeremiah	Joel	Habakkuk
Lamentations	Amos	Zephaniah
Ezekiel	Obadiah	Haggai
Daniel	Jonah	Zechariah
Revelation	Micah	Malachi

Prophecy and Revelation—Judgment with Hope

We include the Book of Revelation in this category because it also is prophetic in nature. The twelve "minor" prophets are so called, not because their message was inferior, but because of their brevity.

Unique Features of Prophetic Literature
The classic passage used to define a prophet is Deuteronomy 18:18.

> *I will raise up for them a prophet like you from among their brothers; I will put my words in his mouth, and he will tell them everything I command him. If anyone does not listen to My words that the prophet speaks in My name, I Myself will call him to account.*

A prophet then is "one who speaks directly for God."

Throughout the Old Testament there were prophets who spoke for God. Generally, we know more about what these prophets *did* than what they *said*, and what they said was placed very specifically in the context of their times. But in the prophetic books, our attention is turned away from the messenger and onto the message. When studying prophetic books, we need to understand *why* they spoke, *when* they spoke, and *what* they spoke.

Why the Prophets Spoke
The key to interpreting the Old Testament prophetic books is to understand how the Mosaic covenant was central to the nation of Israel. The Mosaic covenant was the charter of the nation—a constitution of sorts. It was a legal agreement between Israel and God, constituting Israel as God's chosen people, and placing on them the responsibility of honoring, worshiping, and obeying Yahweh alone. God sent the prophets throughout Israel's history to call the people back to that covenant.

By virtue of this agreement, God was the supreme and absolute King of Israel. But the Israelites didn't live up to their end of the agreement with God. Because of their disobedience, God condemned them to wander in the wilderness for forty years. When they finally did enter the Promised Land, they failed to drive out the pagan nations as God had commanded them. Consequently, they fell into idolatry. We see the results of their continued disobedience during the period of the Judges—a perpetual cycle of apostasy and judgment. Instead of ruling Israel directly, God appointed these judges to rule over His people and help them maintain their covenant faithfulness. But because of Israel's rebellious heart, this form of leadership also failed. God's people were faithful to the covenant only as long as the judge himself was alive. As soon as the judge died, the people fell back into apostasy. So God appointed kings as leaders. After the third king (Solomon), the country erupted into civil war. This war spawned a permanent division: the Northern

Observe Interpret Apply

THREE PERIODS OF THE PROPHETS

① PREEXILIC — ASSYRIAN CAPTIVITY 722 B.C.
② EXILIC — BABYLONIAN CAPTIVITY 586 B.C.
③ POSTEXILIC

ISRAEL: JONAH, AMOS, HOSEA

JUDAH: OBADIAH, JOEL, ISAIAH, MICAH, NAHUM, ZEPHANIAH, HABAKKUK, JEREMIAH

DANIEL, EZEKIEL

RESTORED JUDAH–ISRAEL: HAGGAI, ZECHARIAH, MALACHI

Kingdom called Israel and the Southern Kingdom called Judah. Each of these countries later suffered defeat and deportation by hostile neighbors. Only Judah eventually returned to the homeland.

When the Prophets Spoke

All of the prophetic books were written during the period of the Divided Kingdom. Pages 154, 156–157 show three summary charts that will help put these writings in historical perspective. *Three Periods of the Prophets* shows when the prophets spoke in relation to the Assyrian and Babylonian Captivities. *The Kings and Prophets* (spread over two pages) shows the times of the prophets' ministries and indicates, with dates, the kings who ruled.

What the Prophets Spoke

The king's duty was to keep the nation faithful to its covenant with Yahweh. Because they failed, God raised up prophets to call the nation back to Himself. All of the elements of prophecy are related to this central purpose. It's tempting to translate prophetic messages directly to our own era. God's overarching principles remain the same, but we must remember that particular prophecies were addressed to the people of that time. The overriding message of the prophets can be summarized as:

1. Calling the nation back to covenant faithfulness.

2. Condemning the nation when it refused to repent.

3. Consoling the condemned nation with promises of God's future blessings.

Revelation

Although there are prophetic statements found elsewhere in the New Testament, the Book of Revelation comes closest to fitting our definition of prophetic books. John is told to

Write, therefore, what you have seen, what is now and what will take place later.
—Revelation 1:19

Notice how similar the need and message of Revelation are to those of the Old Testament prophets.

Though the messages in Revelation vary from church to church according to the conditions of each church, a common thread runs through them: remain faithful to God. The repeated phrase "the one who overcomes" refers to this message. From the first four chapters it is clear that, just as the Old Testament prophets exhorted Israel to be faithful

Prophecy and Revelation — Judgment with Hope

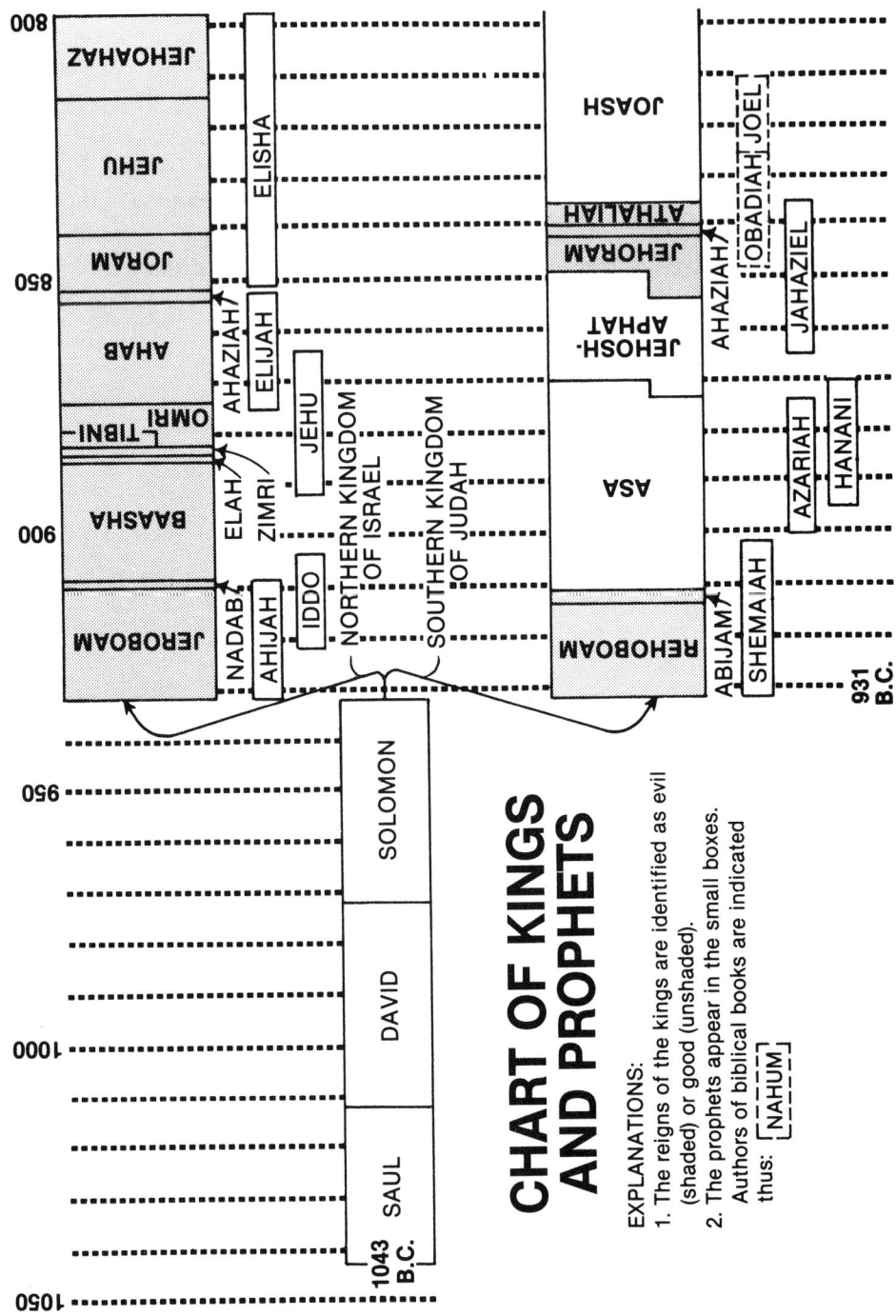

Observe Interpret Apply

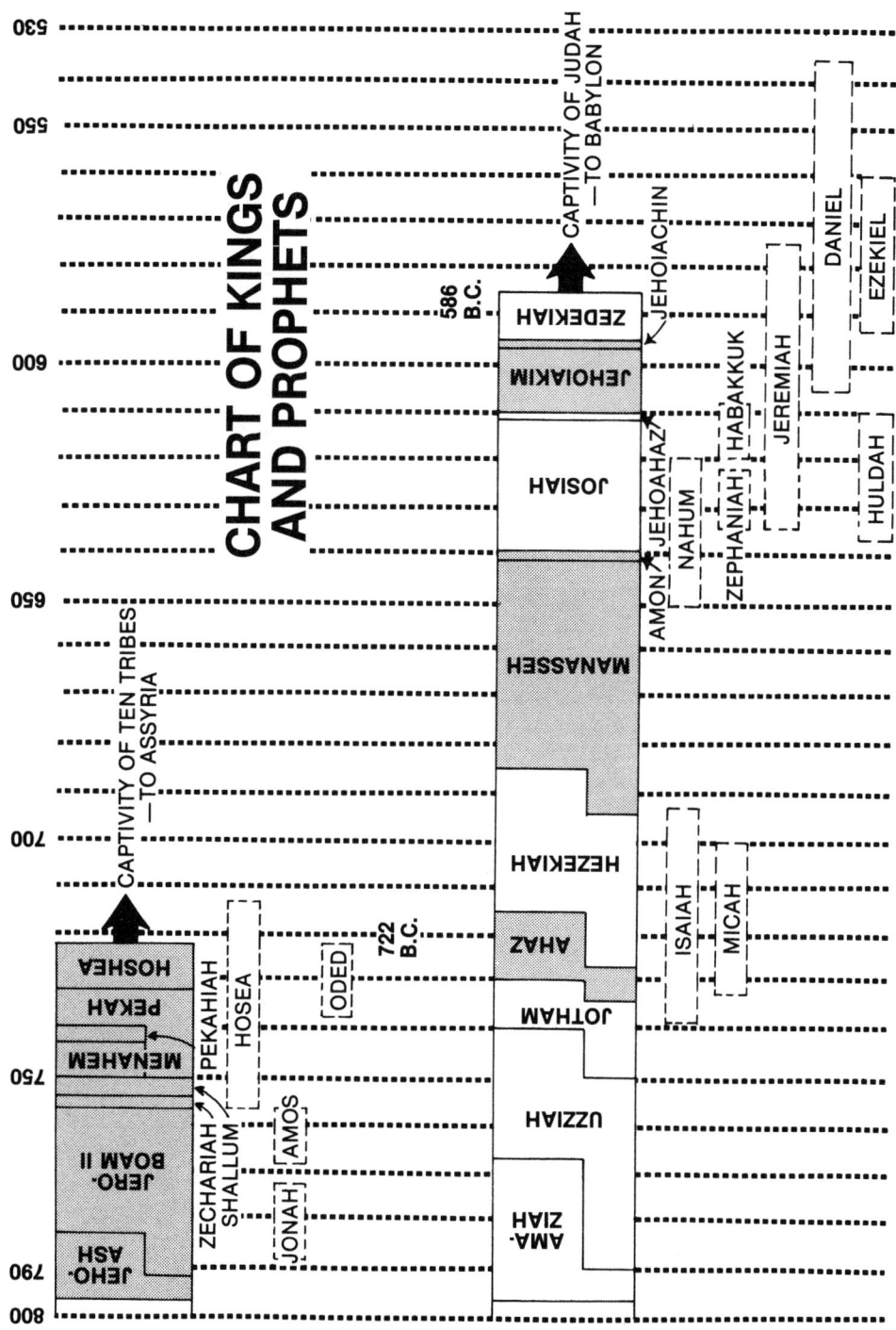

to God, so John is told to call the church to remain faithful to Jesus Christ until He returns.

In the Old Testament, the prophets spoke of God's judgment and blessing on the nation of Israel. John's revelation speaks of God's future judgment and blessing on the churches. To those who are faithful to Christ—those who overcome—there will be rewards, but for those who are unrepentant and disobedient, there will be judgment. Furthermore, like the Old Testament prophets, John speaks of a time when God will cast down all of His enemies, and those of His people, and He will reward the faithful with everlasting blessing.

Many of the symbols and images John uses are taken directly from the prophets. It is important to remember that the cryptic symbolism of chapters 4–22 is not meant to be a detailed description of the end times. If God had intended to give us a clear picture of what the future would hold, it is unlikely that He would have used so many unclear figures and images to describe those events. The meaning of the symbols, taken individually, is not really the concern. The meaning that emerges when all of the images are combined is what is important.

> We need to learn that pictures of the future are just that—pictures. The pictures express a reality but they are not themselves to be confused with reality, nor are the details of every picture necessarily to be "fulfilled" in some specific way. Thus when the first four trumpets proclaim calamities on nature as part of God's judgment, we must not necessarily expect a literal fulfillment of those pictures.[1]

The message of Revelation emerges from these pictures in sharp focus: God will one day defeat all of His enemies in heaven and on earth. He will return in triumph and glory and His saints will share in His victory and receive the reward of eternal blessing and glory.

A Word of Caution about Prophetic Literature
Some people are fascinated with trying to predict future events by unlocking the secrets of the prophets. It's important to understand that the prophets' message was directed primarily to the nation of Israel, not to the church. Although we find principles in the prophetic books which apply to us today, we must be careful not to take the promises and warnings addressed to Israel and apply them directly to the church. The church operates under the *New* Covenant established by Jesus Christ.

The prophets did announce the future. But to see the prophets primarily as predictors of future events misses their primary function: speaking for God to their contemporaries. For us to see their prophecies fulfilled, we must look back on times which for them were still future, but for us are past. Avoid the temptation to see predictive significance in every statement made by the prophets just because those statements occur in prophetic literature. Fee and Stuart comment:

> The primary difficulty for most modern readers of the prophets stems from an inaccurate prior understanding of the word prophecy. For most people this word means what appears as the first definition in most dictionaries: "Foretelling or predicting of what is to come." It often happens, therefore, that many Christians refer to the prophets only for predictions about the coming of Jesus and/or certain features of the New Covenant age—as though prediction of events far distant from their own day was the main concern of the prophets. In fact, using the prophets this way is highly selective. Consider in this connection the following statistics: Less than 2 percent of Old Testament prophecy is messianic. Less than 5 percent specifically describes the New Covenant age. Less than 1 percent concerns events yet to come.[2]

Observing Prophetic Literature

Let's begin our study of prophetic books by surveying a book for the "big picture," not focusing here on details. Examples are provided from several prophetic books as illustrations. When it's your turn to practice studying a prophetic book, you will look at the Minor Prophet Micah.

Observing the Whole

Inductive study of prophetic books helps us understand the nature of this particular type of biblical literature.

> By the very nature of things, we modern readers will find it much harder to understand in our own time the Word of God as it was spoken by the prophets than did the Israelites who heard those same words in person. Things clear to them tend to be opaque to us. Why? Partly, it is because those in a speaker's audience have certain obvious advantages over those who read a speaker's words secondhand. . . . But that is not really where the difficulties lie for the most part. Rather, as people far removed from the religious, historical, and cultural life of ancient Israel, we simply have great trouble putting the words spoken by the prophets in their proper context. It is often hard for us to see what they are referring to and why.[3]

In light of the historical nature of the prophets, it is essential that we investigate the situation the author was addressing. Just as with epistles, you'll need to spend some extra time researching the historical background of that book.

1. Read the book carefully. Read first to get the broad scope of the book. Since the twelve minor prophets are quite short, you can easily read through them in one sitting. The five major prophets and the Book of Revelation are much longer, and will probably require several sittings, much like narratives.

2. Record your initial impressions. As you get an overview of a prophetic book in your reading, take time to reflect on it and record your initial impressions. You may want to scan the longer prophetic books for their major themes and contents before taking a closer look. Take notes about the tone and content of the book, as in the example below.

> **Example from the Book of Lamentations:**
>
> This prophetic book communicates a tone of great sadness, and is devoted primarily to the prophet's expression of regret and sorrow over the disobedience of God's people. We do find, however, that in the midst of this sorrow there is comfort and hope.

As you read a prophetic book, look for answers to:

Who? (the major characters)
What? (the major events and themes)
Where? (the major geographical locations)
When? (the major periods of time)

3. Research the setting. Go back and take a closer look at the historical setting, the occasion of the book. You can begin finding the book's historical and geographical setting in the charts on pages 154, 156–157. Then you can dig deeper into the questions outlined in the previous step. The following elements in a prophetic book — all of which deal with the life of Israel and Judah at the time the prophecy was given — will surface as you look in these places suggested for finding answers to the four questions listed below:

Who? Who are the people involved in this book? Who is this book meant for — Israel, Judah, both? What do we know about these people? Which kings are ruling at the time of the book's writing, and what are they like? What do we learn about the author by reading the book?

Look in:
- ☐ The prophetic book itself
- ☐ The Books of 1 and 2 Kings (tell the political history of the times)
- ☐ The Books of 1 and 2 Chronicles (tell the theological history of the times)

What? What are the key events or ideas in this book? What problems or issues does this book speak to? What is the book's primary teaching? How significant is the content of this particular book in comparison to the others? What atmosphere (feeling) and tone does the book communicate?

Prophecy and Revelation—Judgment with Hope

Look in:
- ☐ The prophetic book itself

Where? Where is the action of this book taking place? What can we learn about the physical and geographical setting and location that helps us understand the book better? Try to locate on a map where the main events of the book took place.

Look in:
- ☐ The prophetic book itself
- ☐ The Books of 1 and 2 Kings (fill in the history and geography of the times)
- ☐ The Books of 1 and 2 Chronicles (also fill in the history and geography of the times)
- ☐ A Bible atlas or maps

When? When was the book written? When do the events take place? What is happening in the lives of the recipients? Is anything said about the author's situation when he was writing? When in the life of Israel and Judah does the action take place?

Look in:
- ☐ The prophetic book itself
- ☐ The Books of 1 and 2 Kings, 1 and 2 Chronicles
- ☐ Time lines of the era

4. Become familiar with the kings of Israel and Judah. Most of the prophets begin by mentioning the reigning king under whom the prophetic oracle is spoken. As the history of the book progresses, the prophet often mentions the new kings who come into power, adding to our sense of history. For example, the book of Isaiah opens with these words:

The vision concerning Judah and Jerusalem that Isaiah son of Amoz saw during the reigns of Uzziah, Jotham, Ahaz, and Hezekiah, kings of Judah.

Then in Isaiah 36:1, he gives us an update of the historical setting.

In the fourteenth year of King Hezekiah's reign, Sennacherib king of Assyria attacked all the fortified cities of Judah and captured them.

The charts on the following pages can help you locate the histories of the kings of Judah in the Books of Kings and Chronicles. For similar information about the kings of Israel, see *Jensen's Bible Study Charts* and John Bright's *A History of Israel* as noted in Appendix B.

Observe Interpret Apply

KINGS OF JUDAH (1–10)

KINGS OF JUDAH	AGE BEGAN REIGNING	YEARS OF REIGN	CHARACTER	RELATIONS WITH ISRAEL	HISTORY
1 REHOBOAM	41	17	BAD	WAR	1 KINGS 12:1–14:31 2 CHRONICLES 10:1–12:16
2 ABIJAM		3	BAD	WAR	1 KINGS 15:1-8 2 CHRONICLES 13:1-22
3 ASA		41	GOOD	WAR	1 KINGS 15:9-24 2 CHRONICLES 14:1–16:14
4 JEHOSHAPHAT	35	25	GOOD	PEACE	1 KINGS 22:41-50 2 CHRONICLES 17:1–20:37
5 JEHORAM	32	8	BAD	PEACE	2 KINGS 8:16-24 2 CHRONICLES 21:1-20
6 AHAZIAH	22	1	BAD	ALLIANCE	2 KINGS 8:25-29; 9:27-29 2 CHRONICLES 22:1-9
7 ATHALIAH (queen)		6	BAD	PEACE	2 KINGS 8:18; 25-28; 11:1-20 2 CHRONICLES 22:1–23:21; 24:7
8 JOASH	7	40	GOOD	PEACE	2 KINGS 11:1–12:21 2 CHRONICLES 22:10–24:27
9 AMAZIAH	25	29	GOOD	WAR	2 KINGS 14:1-14 2 CHRONICLES 25:1-28
10 UZZIAH (Azariah)	16	52	GOOD	PEACE	2 KINGS 15:1-7 2 CHRONICLES 26:1-23

Taken from: *Jensen's Bible Study Charts* (Volume 2), by Irving Jensen. Copyright 1981, Moody Bible Institute of Chicago. Moody Press. Used by permission.

Prophecy and Revelation — Judgment with Hope

KINGS OF JUDAH (11-20)

KINGS OF JUDAH	AGE BEGAN REIGNING	YEARS OF REIGN	CHARACTER	RELATIONS WITH ISRAEL	HISTORY
11 JOTHAM	25	16	GOOD	WAR	2 KINGS 15:32-38 2 CHRONICLES 27:1-9
12 AHAZ	20	16	BAD	WAR	2 KINGS 16:1-20 2 CHRONICLES 28:1-27
13 HEZEKIAH	25	29	GOOD		2 KINGS 18:1-20:21 2 CHRONICLES 29:1-32:33
14 MANASSEH	12	55	BAD		2 KINGS 21:1-18 2 CHRONICLES 33:1-20
15 AMON	22	2	BAD		2 KINGS 21:19-23 2 CHRONICLES 33:21-25
16 JOSIAH	8	31	GOOD		2 KINGS 22:1-23:30 2 CHRONICLES 34:1-35:27
17 JEHOAHAZ	23	3 MOS.	BAD		2 KINGS 23:31-33 2 CHRONICLES 36:1-4
18 JEHOIAKIM	25	11	BAD		2 KINGS 23:34-24:5 2 CHRONICLES 36:5-7
19 JEHOIACHIN	18	3 MOS.	BAD		2 KINGS 24:6-16 2 CHRONICLES 36:8-10
20 ZEDEKIAH	21	11	BAD		2 KINGS 24:17-25:7 2 CHRONICLES 36:11-21

Taken from: *Jensen's Bible Study Charts* (Volume 2), by Irving Jensen. Copyright 1981, Moody Bible Institute of Chicago, Moody Press. Used by permission.

Example: The Book of Jeremiah

The following information illustrates how to study the background of a prophetic book—looking only in the Bible—and find rich material to help understand the book as a whole. In this instance, we have used the Book of Jeremiah to show you how you can study the *who* (the characters) part of the book.

Who? (the setting)

The Writer: Jeremiah

Summary of the author and his circumstances:

1:1	Was a priest
1:4-10	His call
1:10	His ministry
12:1	Was a sensitive man who questioned God
15:15-18	
20:7-9, 14-15	
11:18-19	God uses hardship to make him an iron pillar; a man of God
18:18	
20:2	
26:10-11	
37:11-15	
38:4-6	
39:11-12	

The Recipients: The people of Judah, under the reign of five kings

The first of the five kings was good, but things grew more and more wicked until the final judgment under Babylon in 586 B.C.

King	Spiritual Condition	Years of Reign
Josiah	Good	31 years
Jehoahaz	Bad	3 months
Jehoiakim	Bad	11 years
Jehoiachin	Bad	3 months
Zedekiah	Bad	11 years

Prophecy and Revelation—Judgment with Hope

Observing the Parts

Chartmaking is one of the best ways to observe the structure (or parts) of a book, and in the prophetic books where the structures are interesting and clearly definable, this exercise is particularly fruitful. Making charts of the major prophets in particular will help you understand what might otherwise seem to be long and difficult prophetic utterances.

1. Make an initial chart. The chart will be most similar to those you made for narratives (chapter 12). Your goal is to summarize the major contents for each chapter of the book you are studying. [Hint: You will often find clear divisions between the reigns of different kings and different themes in the prophetic utterance.]

2. Mark the structure. On your chart, mark the principles of structure (see Appendix C).

3. Summarize your findings. Your final chart should be easy to read and reflect the major divisions and structure of the book.

YOUR TURN

Now practice observing a prophetic book with the Book of Micah. First, record your impressions of the book as a whole. Next chart its structure, defining its parts on your first draft. Then revise your findings into a final chart.

Observing the whole: Record your initial impressions, answering the four key questions—*who, what, where,* and *when.* (Approximate time: 2 hours)

Who? (the author and his characteristics)

Observe Interpret Apply

Who? (the recipients and their needs)

What?

Where?

When?

Observing the parts: Make an observational chart of Micah. Create a first draft and mark the principles of structure (see Appendix C). Then, draw a revised chart. (Approximate time: 90 minutes)

BOOK CHART OF MICAH
First draft

Observe Interpret Apply

BOOK CHART OF MICAH
Final draft

Prophecy and Revelation—Judgment with Hope

Interpreting Prophetic Literature

When interpreting prophetic books, it helps to understand that there are four points to which the prophets pointed: the Assyrian and Babylonian captivities, the first coming of Christ, the Second Coming of Christ, and the Millennium. As we noted earlier, less than one percent of Old Testament prophecy concerns the Second Coming of Christ and the Millennium. Conversely, the Book of Revelation concerns itself almost entirely with these events.

Interpreting the Book of Revelation

Because of the unusual character and complexity of the Book of Revelation, there have been four main ways of interpreting it. One's understanding of the events of the book and when they come to pass depends on which school of interpretation one follows.

Preterist. This is from the Latin word meaning "past." This view denies the future predictive quality of most of Revelation holding that the events have already been fulfilled in early church history. Preterists see Revelation 5–11 as the church's victory over Judaism, chapters 12–19 as its victory over pagan Rome, and 20–22 as its glory because of those victories.

Historical. This view holds that the prophecies of Revelation have been in the process of being fulfilled throughout the Christian era. According to this view the various symbols in the book point to the rise of the papacy, the corruption of the church, and various church wars throughout history.

Allegorical. This interpretation grew up in the Alexandrian school of theology in the third and fourth centuries. It views Revelation as an unfolding picture of great principles in constant conflict. It spiritualizes and allegorizes the text, and does not link the events of Revelation with specific historical events.

Futurist or plain interpretation. This is the view adopted by most conservative and premillennial scholars who believe chapters 4–22 of Revelation deal with events yet to come. Futurists believe that chapters 4–18 describe the last seven years preceding the Second Coming of Christ, chapter 19 the Second Coming, chapter 20 the Millennium, and chapters 21–22 the eternal state. This view is held by many today because no judgments in history seem to equal those described in chapters 6, 8–9, and 16. Also, the resurrections and judgments in chapter 20 have not yet occurred, nor has the visible return of Christ portrayed in chapter 19. Your interpretation of the Book of Revelation will depend on how you view the questions outlined above.

The same two questions you have asked of the other genres need to be asked of prophetic books as well: what are the reader's *needs* and what is the writer's *message?* Once again, you answer these questions by following the five C's:

Observe Interpret Apply

1. State an initial proposal based on the content. Your interpretation should arise out of the prophetic book you are studying. Try to state the need and the message of the book in one sentence each.

2. Search the context. In the case of prophetic books of the Old Testament, the writings of the other prophets who preached during the same time in history should be considered the immediate context. The Book of Revelation stands alone in the New Testament; no other New Testament book sheds much light on its meaning.

3. Seek comparison. Let cross references, other Old and New Testament books, and various Bible translations add to your understanding of the book you are studying. Note how often the Old Testament prophets are quoted in the New Testament and how they help you understand the prophet's message.

4. Survey/consult the secondary sources. Because of the historical distance between us and the prophets, and because the language of the prophetic books is at times confusing, it is helpful to consult secondary sources to better understand the purpose of the prophet's message. Bible dictionaries, commentaries, and Bible atlases are valuable sources of information when studying the prophets (see Appendix A).

5. State your conclusions. Now restate your initial interpretive sentences in light of your added insight.

Example: Book of Hosea

▶ *The Need:* Hosea is written to the Northern Kingdom (Israel) around 710 B.C., a decade before it fell into the hands of the Assyrians. The problem is that the people of Israel are faithless to God. They are compared to a marriage where one partner abandons the other. Israel needs to return to Yahweh with whom she has made a covenant.

▶ *The Message:* The message of Hosea could be summarized as: God's love for Israel is steadfast, despite her unfaithfulness. Even though the people of Israel have left God to follow idolatry, God remains willing to forgive them and take them back. This message is illustrated in the marriage of Hosea and Gomer.

Prophecy and Revelation—Judgment with Hope

YOUR TURN

Make an initial proposal now as to the purpose of the Book of Micah. Then go through the other steps for finding the answers for interpretation, filling in the spaces which follow. (Approximate time: 2 hours)

1. Initial Proposal—Study the content. Give your initial responses to these two questions, writing each one in a sentence or two.

▶ *The Readers' Need:*

▶ *The Author's Message:*

2. Search the context and seek comparison. What do other books of the Bible add to your understanding of the message of Micah?

3. Survey/consult the secondary sources. What do commentaries or other Bible study tools say about the purpose of Micah? Write down several key statements you discovered from other writings that helped you understand it better.

Observe Interpret Apply

4. State your conclusions. In light of your findings, how might you revise your initial proposal? Restate your interpretive statements below.

▶ *The Readers' Need:*

▶ *The Author's Message:*

Applying Prophetic Literature

The prophetic books contain rich teaching for us today. For instance, they teach us about God's love in spite of human faithlessness. For someone struggling with forgiveness and the love of God, these books can be of great encouragement. Of course they also teach us about the anger and justice of God concerning sin in our lives.

As you begin this final phase of study in the prophets, keep in mind that you are summarizing your discoveries and looking for principles that relate to daily life. Your applications should arise naturally out of your observation and interpretation of Micah. The four principles of application that follow are familiar by now.

1. Know yourself. What needs in your own life stand out as you are studying the book?

2. Relate the book to life. In light of the series of new relationships (p. 75), what specific application principles come to mind as you think of the prophetic book you are studying?

3. Meditate on the results. Concentrate on finding one key verse as you study. Then think about what it says throughout the day and ask God to make it a part of your life.

4. Practice your findings. Ask yourself, "How can I respond based on what I've learned?" Then write down a specific action to take.

Prophecy and Revelation—Judgment with Hope

YOUR TURN

Write five application principles you find in the Book of Micah. Try to make them personal. (Approximate time: 30 minutes)

Five application principles:

What one action will you take this week to apply one of these principles in your life? Be specific.

CHAPTER 16
How to Study a Topic

I can identify with a man like Joseph. He loved God and tried to serve Him. One day his brothers turned on him and abandoned him. But Joseph resolved not to indulge in bitterness but to be faithful to God. I studied the example of Joseph at a time when my "brothers" abandoned me. Of course, I felt discouraged. But the story of Joseph helped me stay faithful to God during those difficult days.

We have been studying the various genres in Scripture, learning how to observe, interpret, and apply different kinds of literature. In these last chapters, we will discuss how to apply the inductive approach to studying a topic, person, word, or doctrine.

Many biblical preachers and teachers have used a topical method to study Scripture: Jesus (Luke 24:13-27); Peter (Acts 2:1-41); Stephen (Acts 7:1-53); Philip (Acts 8:26-35); and Paul (Acts 26:1-23).

In topical Bible study secondary resources are especially important because we are tracing topics through Scripture. A modern Bible translation with cross references and a concordance are essential. (See Appendixes A and B for additional study resources and their uses.)

Why Study the Bible Topically?
Topical Bible study is a practical way to address unique life and ministry needs. If you or someone you know is facing a special problem, Scripture has something to say on the subject—either directly or in principle. There is no limit to the ways in which the Bible helps us meet the demands and concerns of everyday life.

POSSIBLE STUDY TOPICS

Concepts. This is a general category, covering any subject you would like to trace through the Bible. Some of the topics listed below fall under this general heading. One concept you might study is love.

Doctrine/Theology. This type of study allows you to see systematically what the Bible has to say about a specific theological issue. The deity of Christ is an example of a theological study.

History. Learn all you can about a specific period in Bible history. This type of study examines important biblical dates, individuals, and political events of a particular period in history. An example would be the history of the Children of Israel during their stay in Egypt.

Geography. This type of study involves coming to a thorough understanding of the physical locations of the events in a biblical study. It includes studying maps of cities, countries, and routes of travel. A study of Paul's missionary journeys is an example of a geographical study.

Biographies. Character studies of individuals in the Bible are a popular type of topical Bible study. A study of David's life is an example of a biographical study.

Words. Perhaps you would like to know what the Bible as a whole teaches about faith. You would examine all the instances where that word occurs.

Sermons. The Bible contains numerous sermons available for our study. An example would be the six sermons of Paul in the Book of Acts or the sermons of Jesus in the Gospels.

Miracles. The Bible is a book of God's miraculous activities in human history, from the Garden of Eden to the end of Revelation. You could study the miracles in a particular book or in a specific period of time in the history of God's people or even in a particular person's life. Perhaps the most obvious topical study of this type would be the miracles of Jesus.

Attributes of God. One of the most important studies we can do is to study who God is. As you look at a particular book of the Bible, keep this question in mind: "What can I learn about what God is like from this book?"

Jesus Christ. The person and work of Jesus Christ is evident throughout the Bible. You might study the prophecies about Christ found in the Old Testament or the life of Christ in the Gospels.

Holy Spirit. Trace the work and ministry of the Holy Spirit throughout the Old and New Testaments or examine the deity of the Holy Spirit.

Parables. Have you ever done a topical study on the parables of Jesus? Sometime you might want to trace the principles of the parables throughout the Gospels.

Prophecies. Learning the overall scheme of events that the prophets predicted makes for fascinating study. You could study the Old Testament prophecies that led up to the first coming of Christ, and contrast those with the New Testament predictions of His Second Coming.

Prayers. The Bible records many of the prayers of God's people. These prayers can help us in our own praying. You could look at Paul's prayers in the epistles.

Commands. There are many admonitions in Scripture that are meant for us personally. Studying the commands of the Bible will help us understand what our responsibility is before God. It will also help us clarify and better understand how to do God's will.

Promises. You could fill a notebook with the promises from God's Word. This type of study is wonderful for meditation.

Conversions. The testimony of personal conversions is a strong witness to the unbeliever, and Scripture records a number of them. If you have a special interest in evangelism, you may want to analyze some of the conversions recorded in Scripture. In your study, see what led to the conversions and what they teach us about leading others to Christ.

Revivals. There are periods of history recorded throughout Scripture that tell us about the spiritual high points of God's dealing with men and women. Find out all you can about these "revivals" and how their teachings can encourage us today.

The Bible. Does it seem strange that the Bible would have so much to say about itself? God wants us to understand the importance of His Word in our lives. Sometime, try analyzing what Scripture has to say about its own integrity and authority in your life.

How to Study a Topic

Perhaps you're interested in studying the miracles of Jesus in the Gospel of John, or what the Book of Proverbs has to say on the use of the tongue, or the "I am" sayings of Jesus in the Gospels. Any of these topical studies would be of great spiritual benefit. The topics and themes are endless—you'll never run out of new ways to look at God's Word to us!

Study pages 175-176. This is only a partial list of topics one could study in the Bible. Let this list whet your appetite for topical study and stimulate your own creative thinking about topics you can study in Scripture.

Topics in Specific Books
Before moving on to the actual process of studying a topic, we need to mention one more thing about what to study. You will recall that there are five major genres, or types of literature in the Bible. Can you name them from memory? (If necessary, refer to page 83.)

The five major genres of biblical literature:

1.

2.

3.

4.

5.

When studying the Bible topically within individual books, there are certain subjects to concentrate on, depending on the genre. In the spaces that follow, list several subjects you think would be important topical studies for each type of literature. (Try not to look ahead at the answers.)

1.

2.

3.

4.

5.

Observe Interpret Apply

Here is a brief summary of topics you might consider studying in each of the genres.

Topics in Narratives

When studying historical books topically, look at what the entire book has to say about:
- ☐ Key characters (David in 1 Samuel)
- ☐ Repeated key events (God speaking to Abraham in Genesis)
- ☐ Major themes or concepts (miracles in the Gospels)
- ☐ Sermons (Paul's messages in Acts)
- ☐ Prayers (the prayers of Jesus)
- ☐ Places mentioned repeatedly (Mount Zion)
- ☐ Key buildings (the tabernacle)
- ☐ Key cities (Jericho in Joshua)
- ☐ Key nations (Egypt in the Old Testament)
- ☐ Key landmarks (burial places in the Old Testament)

Topics in Epistles

When observing the Epistles topically, look for:
- ☐ Key words
- ☐ Commands
- ☐ Promises
- ☐ Warnings
- ☐ Recurring concepts
- ☐ Doctrines

Topics in Wisdom and Poetry Books

Because there are only a few of these books, each is treated separately.

Job:
- ☐ Pain and suffering
- ☐ The attributes of God
- ☐ God's concept of Himself
- ☐ Character traits of friends
- ☐ Friends' concept of God

Psalms:
- ☐ The nature of worship
- ☐ The attributes of God
- ☐ The nature of praise
- ☐ Sin and its consequences
- ☐ Confession
- ☐ The Messiah
- ☐ Joy and peace
- ☐ How and what to pray
- ☐ Enemies
- ☐ The promises of God
- ☐ The Word of God

Song of Solomon:
(There is one major theme in the Song of Solomon—the love between a man and woman.)
- ☐ Attitudes of the man
- ☐ His actions of love
- ☐ True love between a man and woman
- ☐ Attitudes of the woman
- ☐ Her response of love

How to Study a Topic

Proverbs:

- ☐ Use of the tongue
- ☐ Use of money
- ☐ Marriage
- ☐ Child rearing
- ☐ Relationships between men and women
- ☐ Friendship
- ☐ Work and laziness
- ☐ Morality
- ☐ Folly

Ecclesiastes:

- ☐ The vain pursuits of life
- ☐ The source of meaning in life
- ☐ The attributes of God
- ☐ The real purpose of life

Topics in Prophetic Books

Valuable topics in prophetic books are:

- ☐ Warnings
- ☐ Promises
- ☐ The attributes of God
- ☐ Figures of speech
- ☐ Prophecies about Jesus Christ
- ☐ Judgment and punishment
- ☐ Forgiveness and healing
- ☐ The prophets themselves
- ☐ Visions
- ☐ God's omnipotence

Observing a Topic

Now that you know some of the important topics for study, let's get down to the specifics of topical study. We will first explain the method, then demonstrate it by using an example from Scripture, and finally you will practice studying a topic of your choice from the Book of Genesis. The sample study looks at the concept of *unity*.

In topical Bible study, observation follows five steps which are similar to those you learned in Part One. Topical studies, however, require a few modifications.

Step 1: Select your subject

Step 2: Gather all the data

Step 3. Reflect on your findings

Step 4: Organize your findings

Step 5: Choose the primary passage

1. Select your subject. Your first task in topical Bible study is to choose a subject. It may be a subject already mentioned here or one of your own choosing. Often, studying one portion of Scripture brings to mind something else you'd like to study. So make note of other possible topics for future study.

2. Gather all the data. Once you've selected your subject, gather all the facts you can about it. If you're studying a topic within a particular book, your research will be limited to that book. If you are studying a broader subject, like *unity,* you'll want to look throughout Scripture.

Here is where a Bible translation with good cross-references and a concordance are essential tools. Look up every occurrence of your topic that is listed in the concordance. At this point, you are simply listing what you find as you discover it—you'll organize it later. If you are studying a broad subject like *love,* you may need to be selective about which verses you read, since that word occurs in such abundance throughout Scripture. Another valuable source at this stage is a topical Bible. These books print significant portions of Scripture under each topic and list additional references at the end of each category. *Nave's Topical Bible* (Appendix B) is an example. Various computer aids, also listed in Appendix B, will also assist your search through the Scripture for passages that address particular topics.

The following illustration for the word *unity* was taken from *Young's Analytical Concordance to the Bible.* The word *unity* only occurs three times in Scripture—once in the Old Testament and twice in the New Testament—so it is easy to do the beginning research on this topic.

Unity, (together in)—

1. *At one, together.* (Hebrew) *yachad.* Psalm 133:1 "How good and pleasant it is when brothers live together in unity!"
2. *Unity.* (Greek) *henotes.*
   Ephesians 4:3 "make every effort to keep the unity of the Spirit"
   Ephesians 4:13 "until we all reach unity in the faith"

Where else might you find out more about the concept of unity in the Bible? Since this is not a strict word study (covered in chapter 18), you can look up other words that convey similar ideas and concepts. Can you think of any other words that address this topic? One way to do additional investigation is by using cross references.

Below is an example of cross-referencing for the word unity from Ephesians 4. As we trace this word back to other verses in Scripture, we find it is often used in connection with words like *one* and *one another.*

Unity in the Body of Christ

CHAPTER 4

As a prisoner[s] for the Lord, then, I urge you to live a life worthy[t] of the calling[u] you have received. [2]Be completely humble and gentle; be patient, bearing with one another[v] in love.[w] [3]Make every effort to keep the unity[x] of the Spirit through the bond of peace.[y] [4]There is one body[z] and one Spirit[a]—just as you were called to one hope when you were called[b]—[5]one Lord,[c] one faith, one baptism; [6]one God and Father of all,[d] who is over all and through all and in all.[e]

[7]But to each one of us[f] grace[g] has been given[h] as Christ apportioned it. [8]This is why it says:

"When he ascended on high,
he led captives[i] in his train
and gave gifts to men."[j]

[9](What does "he ascended" mean except that he also descended to the lower, earthly regions?[10]He who descended is the very one who ascended[k] higher than all the heavens, in order to fill the whole universe.)[l] [11]It was he who gave[m] some to be apostles,[n] some to be prophets,[o] some to be evangelists,[p] and some to be pastors and teachers,[q] [12]to prepare God's people for works of service, so that the body of Christ[r] may be built up[s] [13]until we all reach unity[t] in the faith and in the knowledge of the Son of God[u] and become mature,[v] attaining to the whole measure of the fullness of Christ.[w]

[14]Then we will no longer be infants,[x] tossed back and forth by the waves,[y] and blown here and there by every wind of teaching and by the cunning and craftiness of men in their deceitful scheming.[z] [15]Instead, speaking the truth in love,[a] we will in all things grow up into him who is the Head,[b] that is, Christ. [16]From him the whole body, joined and held together by every supporting ligament, grows[c] and builds itself up[d] in love,[e] as each part does its work.

4:1 [s]see Eph. 3:1
[t]Phil. 1:27; Col. 1:10; 1 Thes. 2:12
[u]see Rom. 8:28
4:2 [v]Col. 3:12-13
[w]ver. 15, 16; Eph. 1:4
4:3 [x]see Rom. 15:5
[y]Col. 3:15
4:4 [z]see Rom. 12:5
[a]1 Cor. 12:13; Eph. 2:18
[b]see Rom. 8:28
4:5 [c]1 Cor. 8:6
4:6 [d]Deut. 6:4; Zech. 14:9
[e]see Rom. 11:36
4:7 [f]1 Cor. 12:7, 11
[g]see Rom. 3:24
[h]see Rom. 12:3
4:8 [i]Col. 2:15
[j]Ps. 68:18
4:10 [k]Prov. 30:1-4
[l]Eph. 1:23
4:11 [m]ver. 8
[n]1 Cor. 12:28; Eph. 2:20; 3:5; 2 Peter 3:2; Jude 17
[o]see Acts 11:27; Rom. 12:6; 1 Cor. 12:10, 28; 13:2, 8; 14:1, 39; Eph. 2:20; 3:5; 2 Peter 3:2
[p]Acts 21:8; 2 Tim. 4:5
[q]Acts 13:1; Rom. 2:21; 12:7; 1 Cor. 12:28; 14:26; 1 Tim. 1:7; James 3:1
4:12 [r]see 1 Cor. 12:27
[s]see Rom. 14:19
4:13 [t]ver 3, 5
[u]see Phil. 3:8
[v]see 1 Cor. 2:6; Col. 1:28
[w]John 1:16; Eph. 1:23; 3:19
4:14 [x]see 1 Cor. 14:20
[y]Isa. 57:20; James 1:6
[z]Eph. 6:11
4:15 [a]ver. 2, 16; Eph. 1:4
[b]see Eph. 1:22
4:16 [c]Col. 2:19
[d]1 Cor. 12:7 [e]ver 2, 15; Eph. 1:4

Observe Interpret Apply

The next step in gathering data is to trace the cross references and the cross references of each new passage and begin compiling a list of all the related information you find on the subject. For example, many references to the idea of unity occur in the New Testament, especially in Paul's epistles. Though Paul doesn't specifically use the word *unity* often, he does often expresses the idea of "being one."

RELATED INFORMATION ON UNITY

John 17	Unity: Christ's goal for the Church
Acts 4:32	All things in common
Romans 12:4-5, 16;	One body, many parts
14:19;	Build up one another
15:5-6	Be of the same mind
1 Corinthians 1:10;	Agree; no divisions among you
12:12-26	One body, many parts
2 Corinthians 13:11	Be like-minded
Galatians 3:26-28	All sons of God through faith
Ephesians 2:14-18;	One in Christ—preserve unity
4:1-16	Believers united make up the body of Christ
Philippians 1:27;	Be of one mind; work together
2:1-4	Hold one another in high regard; don't be selfish
Colossians 3:12-15	Love: the perfect bond of unity
1 Thessalonians 5:11	Encourage and build up one another
2 Thessalonians 1:3	Your love for one another is growing
1 Peter 3:8	Be harmonious

This is not an exhaustive list of what the Bible says about unity, but it illustrates the important information we can find on the subject as we search Scripture. Always gather all the facts you can about a subject *before* you begin analyzing them.

3. Reflect on your findings. Begin to note your impressions of the material you've found to this point. (This step is similar to what you did earlier when you made your initial observations after reading a passage of Scripture.) Before you actually begin to organize all of your findings and to draw conclusions, take time to stand back and reflect on what you've already learned.

> **Example:**
>
> Having gathered as much data as we can on the subject of unity, we might reflect on our findings in this way:
>
> 1. Though the word *unity* does not appear often in Scripture, it does seem to be an important concept.
> 2. Paul seems particularly concerned about unity.
> 3. Unity seems to characterize a healthy church.
> 4. Unity and love go hand in hand.
> 5. The Church is commanded to have unity.
> 6. Unity relates to the individual Christian and the church.
> 7. Jesus prayed for the unity of His followers just before His death (John 17).

4. Organize your findings. Once you've gathered all the data and reflected on your initial findings, go back and organize the results of your research. Have groups of ideas emerged from the Scriptures you've been studying? Are there differences between what the Old and New Testaments say on the subject? Can you classify the various teachings you've found on the topic?

> **Example:**
>
> Unity is mentioned in both the Old and New Testament. We might organize our findings on unity in this way:
>
> *1. Unity is important.*
>   The fact that there are so many references to the concept of unity in the New Testament shows that it is important. Whenever unity is mentioned, it is seen as an essential characteristic of a mature church.
>
> *2. God is the source of unity.*
>   ☐ Jesus Christ (Galatians 3:28)
>   ☐ Holy Spirit (1 Corinthians 12:13)
>
> *3. We have a responsibility to secure unity.*
>   This is taught particularly in the key passage of Philippians 1:27–2:11. In this passage we see that:
>   ☐ Unity is the goal of the Church (vv. 1-2).
>   ☐ Love produces that unity (vv. 3-4).
>   ☐ Humility is the key to love in the church (v. 5ff).
>   ☐ Jesus is a perfect example of the kind of humility that leads to unity (v. 5ff).

Observe Interpret Apply

5. Choose the primary passage. If someone asked you what the Bible says about love, you would probably think of Paul's words in 1 Corinthians 13. Why? Because love is a key topic in the Bible, and 1 Corinthians 13 is often cited as the key passage on that subject. Finding a primary passage on a given subject is a necessary step in topical Bible study. You may not always be able to isolate one passage or verse that speaks comprehensively on the topic, but you should be able to pick out one that comes closest to reflecting the Bible's teaching on that particular subject. Being able to link topics with primary passages is valuable information to have at your fingertips. Not only does it make locating subjects in Scripture easier, it also helps you summarize the results of your study.

Example:

At least two key passages in the New Testament summarize the importance of unity:

1. John 17 stresses how important Jesus Christ felt unity was for the church. In His prayer, Jesus asked the Father to preserve the church in the bond of unity. He knew that without unity, the world would never believe that He was the Son of God.

2. In terms of teaching on unity in the New Testament, Philippians 2 might be considered the primary passage. In this chapter, we find both the goal of unity and the means of attaining that goal through love and humility.

YOUR TURN

What questions do you have at this point about observing a topic in Scripture?

How to Study a Topic

Interpreting a Topic

Having observed our topic, it's time to clarify the teachings we found on the subject and prepare it for specific application to life. As was the case in observation, the process of interpretation is similar to what you learned in Part One—with a few modifications.

1. State the teaching principles
2. Search the contexts and seek comparisons
3. Survey/Consult the secondary sources
4. State your conclusions

1. State the teaching principles. Begin by making a list of all the principles you have found thus far for the topic you are studying. Ask yourself, "What does this topic have to say that is useful for Christian living and for the church in general?"

> **Example:**
>
> Here is a series of teaching principles based on a study of unity throughout the Bible.
>
> 1. Unity is a high priority for the church of Jesus Christ.
> 2. Without unity, the church cannot be an effective witness for Jesus Christ.
> 3. Unity must be aggressively sought after by each member of the local church.
> 4. The key to unity is love.
> 5. The key to loving one another (which produces unity) is found in the humility of one Christian toward another.
> 6. God has provided us a source for unity through our oneness in the body of Christ and the power of the Holy Spirit.

2. Search the contexts and seek comparisons. Whenever we interpret what the Bible teaches on a given subject, we need to check our thinking with what the rest of Scripture teaches. Is there anything in other parts of Scripture that affects the teaching principles you have stated? Do other biblical doctrines or teachings help qualify your findings? Does the topic you have been studying relate to other areas that you must consider?

> **Example:**
>
> Two subjects that are related to the topic of unity in the New Testament are *love* and *humility*. Any teachings on unity must take into account those two subjects.

3. Survey/consult the secondary sources. What do various study tools add to your understanding of the topic? Do they confirm your ideas? Do they cause you to dig a little deeper in Scripture for alternative ideas on the subject?

> **Example:**
>
> This selection from *Baker's Dictionary of Theology* gives us new insight into the concept of unity in the Bible.
>
> The word unity is, as such, very rare in the Bible, but the thought behind the term, that of "the one people of God," is extremely prominent. Already in the Old Testament Israel is descended from the one father, and although the tribes are later divided, the psalmist commends unity (Ps. 133:1) and Ezekiel looks to the time when there shall be "one stick" (Ezek. 37:17). Nor is this merely a political or natural unity, for Abraham is divinely elected, and Isaac is the child of special promise and miracle.
>
> In the New Testament this unity is expanded in accordance with the original promise. The wall of partition between Jew and Gentile, and indeed between Greeks and barbarians, bond and slave, male and female, is broken down. There is now the one people of God embracing men of all nations (Eph. 2:12ff; Gal. 3:28).
>
> But this new unity is not one of mere good will, or common interests, or ecclesiastical organization. It is a unity of expansion because of contraction. It is a unity in the one seed (Gal. 3:16) who has come as the true Israelite and indeed the Second Adam (Rom. 5:12ff). The old and estranged men are made one in Jesus Christ (Eph. 2:15). The one Jesus Christ is the basis of the unity of His people.[1]

4. State your conclusions. Taking the main point of what you've learned, write a concluding statement of interpretation that summarizes the main teachings of the topic.

> **Example:**
>
> Unity is to be a high priority in Christian responsibility as a member of the body of Christ, as seen through the emphasis given to it by Jesus in John 17 and Paul in his epistles.

Applying a Topic

In the application process, you are summarizing your discoveries and looking for principles to apply to your daily life. As we noted in Part One of this workbook, your applications should arise naturally out of the principles you discovered during your observation and interpretation of the topic.

How to Study a Topic

The same suggestions we've used before to apply Scripture to our lives apply to topical study as well.

1. Know yourself. As you studied this topic, what needs in your own life stood out? Were there certain elements of the topic that struck a particular chord in your heart?

2. Relate the topic to life. Are there specific application principles that come to the forefront as you think in terms of the series of new relationships (p. 75).

3. Meditate on the results. It's helpful to focus on one key verse to apply—perhaps the primary verse you identified earlier for the topic. During the day think about what it says, and ask God to make it a part of your life.

4. Practice your findings. Ask yourself, "What is my response, based on what I've learned here?" Write down a specific step of action you can take and act on it.

YOUR TURN

Now you'll have an opportunity to practice topical Bible study. Refer back to the instructions given earlier if you have questions. [Note: In order to make the discussion of your answers more profitable to others in your group, have everyone choose the same topic from Genesis. If you are not studying in a group, choose any topic you wish.]

Observing a Topic

1. Select your subject. Choose a topic that can be traced through the Book of Genesis. It may be, a theme, prophecies about the nation of Israel, promises, commands, an issue that threads through the book, or the direct conversations between God and His servants.

The subject I/we have chosen to study is: _____.

2. Gather all the data. Search through the Book of Genesis for all the verses that mention your topic. First locate your subject in Genesis by simply reading the book, then use a concordance and cross references. Write your main findings in the space provided (Approximate time: 90 minutes).

How to Study a Topic

3. Reflect on your findings. What impresses you most about what you discovered about this topic? Make a list of at least fifteen impressions you have about this topic and the importance of these impressions. (Approximate time: 20 minutes)

4. Organize your findings. Organize the results of your research into meaningful and logical units. Group together various aspects of teaching on the topic being studied. See page 183 for an example. (Approximate time: 30 minutes)

5. Choose the primary passage. What is the most comprehensive passage you have found on this topic? If you had to choose one key verse on this topic, which one would it be? (Approximate time: 10 minutes)

Interpreting a Topic

1. State the teaching principles. Write at least five principles that you can draw from your study of this topic. See page 185 for examples. (Approximate time: 30 minutes)

2. Search the context and seek comparisons. What do other books of the Bible add to your understanding of this topic? (Approximate time: 30 minutes)

3. *Survey/consult the secondary sources.* Refer to a concordance, commentaries, and Bible dictionaries to see what they have to say about your topic. Summarize a few of your findings in the space provided. (Approximate time: 30 minutes)

4. *State your conclusions.* In light of your findings, what do you think is the major teaching of this topic. (Approximate time: 10 minutes)

How to Study a Topic

Applying a Topic
Write five application principles from your study of this topic. They may be related to the principles you listed on page 191 as "teaching principles." Try to personalize them.

Five application principles:

What one action can you take this week to apply one of these principles in your life? Be specific.

CHAPTER 17
How to Study a Person

Topical Bible studies come in a host of varieties. Three categories, however, come up so often that we've devoted a chapter to each: people, words, and doctrines. As you study these three chapters, keep in mind all the principles and features you learned about topical study in chapter 16.

How to Study a Person

Biographical Bible study is a popular type of topical study. By looking at how God acted in the lives of people in the Bible we can learn a great deal about our own situations. Use the techniques you learned in chapter 16 about general topical studies as you pick up additional information here on how to study the particular topic of biblical characters.

There are over 2,900 characters mentioned in the Bible. Not all of them warrant a complete study; some of them are mentioned only once. There are, however, hundreds of men and women in the Bible whose lives were uniquely touched by God and who deserve our reflection.

> *For everything that was written in the past was written to teach us, so that through endurance and the encouragement of the Scriptures we might have hope.*
> *—Romans 15:4*

> *These things happened to them as examples and were written down as warnings for us, on whom the fulfillment of the ages has come.*
> *—1 Corinthians 10:11*

How to Study a Person

Observing a Person
When observing the life of a Bible character, follow these six steps:

1. Select a character. You can study a character within a particular book or throughout the Bible. We use David as our example here. [Note: Be careful not to confuse different names for the same person. Peter, for example, is also called Simon and Simeon at times. Also, several people in the Bible have the same name—there are fifteen Jonathans, eight Judases, seven Marys, five Jameses, and five Johns.]

2. Gather all the data. Find all of the Scriptures you can on the person's life. For some characters, such as Jesus, or Abraham, or Paul, you will find pages of Scripture that illustrate their lives. For others, you may find only a few passages. Isolate all the significant passages that relate to your character.

In studying the life of David, for example, a concordance helps locate the concentrated sections of material as well as places where he is mentioned only briefly. Make a list of all the important passages in Scripture where your character is mentioned. Then read through those passages to get a broad picture of the person's life.

Example from David's life:

Most of the material that describes David's life is found in 1 and 2 Samuel and 1 and 2 Chronicles. We first become aware of David when he is anointed king (1 Samuel 16). The story of his life continues throughout the remaining chapters of 1 Samuel and through all of 2 Samuel (1 Chronicles 12–29 gives a parallel account). David is also mentioned approximately fifty times in the New Testament. In addition, more than seventy psalms appear under his name.

---

3. Organize your findings. Go back and organize your findings. Look in the areas on page 196 for information on the person.

4. Produce a time line of the person's life. A time line is a helpful way to organize the facts of a person's life. Using a straight line, mark all the major events of the person's life, including the dates when those events took place and the major passages of Scripture that describe those events. Refer to page 197, the sample time line on David's life, for ideas.

Observe Interpret Apply

DATA FOR TIME LINE

Name. What does the Bible character's name mean? A Bible dictionary will help here. The meaning of a name can reveal the person's character and importance.

Birth. What are the facts surrounding the person's birth? Where was he/she born? When? Is there anything unusual about the birth?

Family background. What sort of parents did this person have? What was his/her home life like? What role did this person's parents, brothers, and sisters play?

Early life and training. How did the person's parents and relatives influence his/her early years? Is there anything we can learn about the person's early years of training? Try to uncover the influences and environmental factors that shaped this person's life and thinking (for example, school and religious training).

Conversion. What is known about this person's relationship with God? What influences caused this person to become a believer?

Historical setting. What were the contemporary conditions (social, religious, political, economic) that surrounded this person's life?

Geographical movements. Does geography play a major role in this person's life? Where did he/she live? Did this person move from place to place, or did he/she remain at one location most of the time?

Sin. Are there any instances of sin that stand out in this person's life? What was the nature of the sin? How was (or wasn't) the sin overcome? Future effects?

Spiritual life. How would you describe this person's relationship with God? What was his/her prayer life like? Did this person have a strong or weak faith? Is there a record of any periods of spiritual dryness? Spiritual revival? How did this person's relationship with God affect his/her life and accomplishments?

Major accomplishments. What was this person's crowning achievement and contribution to the the nation of Israel or the cause of Christ? Is this person the author of any of the books of the Bible?

Death. How did this person die? Was there anything unusual about his/her death? Is there a message to be communicated through the person's death?

Major lessons. What are the most important principles for today that emerge from this person's life? Would this person be effective in our world today?

How to Study a Person

TIME LINE OF DAVID'S LIFE

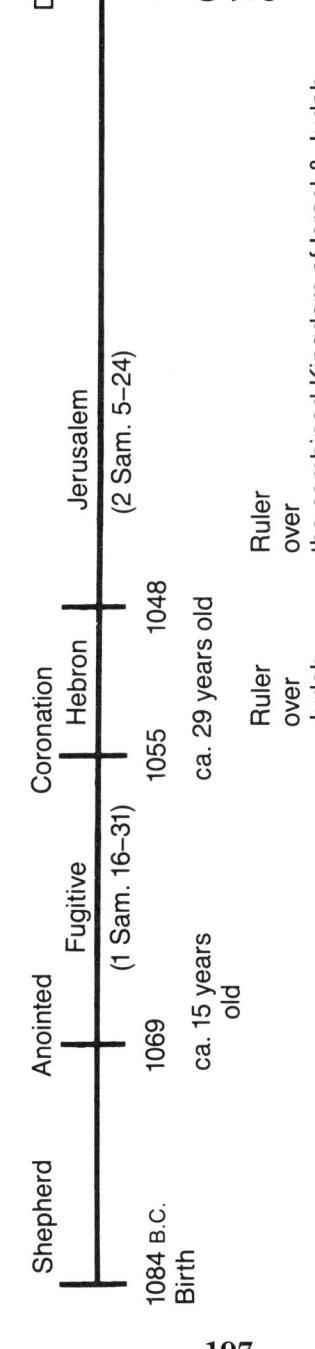

5. Consult secondary sources. What do scholars have to say about the person's life?

6. Choose a primary passage. Choose one passage (or several) that seems to best summarize the character's life. This primary passage should reflect a major implication of this person's life for our lives today.

Interpreting and Applying Biographical Studies
When studying a person, the interpretation and application processes are the same as those described in chapter 16. One special caution regarding biblical character studies: just because a biblical character behaves in a certain way does not mean that we are to copy that behavior. The story itself sometimes condemns certain actions, as it does with David's sin with Bathsheba. But other actions, like Abraham lying about his relationship with his wife, the Bible leaves us to evaluate for ourselves. We should do so—using general principles of morality taught throughout Scripture.

YOUR TURN

Study the characters Priscilla and Aquila. Use as many of the techniques in this chapter as you consider appropriate. Hint: You will find a map and a time line of Paul's life helpful.

CHAPTER 18
How to Study Key Words

Have you ever come across a word in Scripture that you found difficult to understand? Often, it is important to grasp the meaning of a word in order to understand the meaning of the passage in which it occurs. An orderly word study can often shed light on difficult words in the Bible. Use the general information from chapter 16 about how to study a topic as well as particular helps in this chapter.

Before discussing the principles for studying a word, it is important to mention some of the difficulties associated with defining words in Scripture.

1. Words change their meanings. A word that means one thing at a certain point in history often comes to mean something else in subsequent history and in contemporary society. For example, in seventeenth-century England, the word *prevent* meant "to go before." Today, *prevent* means "to stop." These are dramatically different meanings for the same word. Notice how the change affects our understanding of 1 Thessalonians 4:15 if we accidentally insert the contemporary meaning of *prevent.* Instead of "we who are still alive, who are left till the coming of the Lord, will certainly not *precede* those who have fallen asleep," the verse becomes, "will certainly not *stop* those who have fallen asleep." Such is the kind of confusion created by the natural evolution of a word's meaning.

2. Different words have the same meaning. There are often a number of different words that give various shades of meaning to the same idea. For instance, the word *stop* could also be expressed by the words *cease, hinder, quit, desist, finish.* These are synonyms because they have similar meanings. At times, the Bible uses synonyms to express variations of the same thought. Take the word *eternal,* for example. This concept is also expressed in Scripture by the words *forever, everlasting, age,* and *generation after generation,* each with slightly different shades of meaning.

3. The same words have different meanings. The same words can mean different things to different people. If I say I am going to hit the "trunk," I could mean the storage compartment of a car, the nose of an elephant, the core of a tree, or a large suitcase! Let's use the word *heaven* as an example from Scripture. *Heaven* has a number of meanings. In some places it refers to the sky, in others it refers to the heavens (stars, galaxies, outer space). We also know that heaven is where God dwells, where believers will live with Him forever. It is important to determine the meaning of a word as it is meant to be understood in the particular passage or book you are studying.

4. Some Bible words are obscure. Many topics that the Bible deals with are not part of our everyday life today, so it can be difficult to attach meaning to words that are uniquely Christian. Words such as *sanctification, glory, propitiation,* and *atonement* are rarely used in the day-to-day conversations of our secular society — and if they are, their meaning has likely been changed. Their obscurity makes them more difficult to define with modern language.

5. Translation issues can sometimes add to the confusion. The Bible was originally written in ancient Hebrew, Greek, and a small portion in Aramaic. Different Bible translators choose to translate the same Greek or Hebrew word differently. Sometimes a translator's personal convictions determine what meaning and interpretation is given to a word in a particular context. At other times a translation team decides the meaning of words. Translators are people; they are not inspired by God as the original writers were. The problem of translation differences highlights the value of studying words in their original languages.

Context Is the Key
When doing a word study, your goal is simply to find the meaning of the word in the context where it occurs. This principle of context is crucial in any language. Practically any word you look up in the dictionary has a number of meanings. Only the context in which that word is used can tell you which meaning is intended by the author.

The writers of Scripture probably had only one meaning in mind as they wrote their books. Whenever you find a word in Scripture that you don't understand, your goal is to *discover the author's intended meaning* for the word. We assume that most people using this workbook will at least have access to a concordance. (Though not impossible, it is difficult to do precise word studies without knowing the word in its original language.)

How to Study Key Words

1. Find the correct Greek or Hebrew word. Most word studies result from studying a passage of Scripture and finding a word you do not understand. To do an accurate word study, you first need to recognize that the word you want to study was originally a Hebrew or Greek word.

Find the original word by using a concordance that indicates what Greek or Hebrew word is at the root of the word. Look up the word you wish to study in your concordance. Under the entry for that word, you will find a list of references showing every place in the Bible where the word occurs in its various Hebrew and Greek forms. Beside the Scripture references will be brief phrases showing the immediate context of the verse in which the word is used. The example here for the word *reap* is from *Young's Analytical Concordance to the Bible:*

REAP (wholly, down), to —
1. *To finish,* כָּלָה *kalah,* 3.
   Lev. 19. 9 thou shalt not wholly reap the corners of
2. *To shorten, reap,* קָצַר *qatsar.*
   Lev. 19. 9 When ye reap the harvest of your land, th.
      23. 10 When ye..shall reap the harvest thereof
      23. 22 when ye reap the harvest of your land
      23. 22 not make clean riddance..when thou re.
      25. 5 thou shalt not reap, neither gather the g.
      25. 11 neither reap that which groweth of itself
   Ruth 2. 9 thine eyes (be) on the field that they dor.
   1 Sa. 8. 12 and to reap his harvest, and to make his
   2 Ki. 19. 29 reap, and plant vineyards, and eat the fr.
   Job 4. 8 they that..sow wickedness, reap the same
      24. 6 They reap (every one) his corn in the field
   Psa. 126. 5 They that sow in tears shall reap in joy
   Prov. 22. 8 He that soweth iniquity shall reap vanity
   Eccl. 11. 4 he that regardeth the clouds shall not re.
   Isa. 17. 5 reapeth the ears with his arm; and it sh.
      37. 30 reap, and plant vineyards, and eat the fr.
   Jer. 12. 13 They have sown wheat, but shall reap th.
   Hos. 8. 7 they shall reap the whirlwind: it hath no
      10. 12 reap in mercy; break up your fallow gro.
      10. 13 ye have reaped iniquity; ye have eaten the
   Mic. 6. 15 thou shalt not reap; thou shalt tread the
3. *To reap, mow, gather together,* ἀμάω *amaō.*
   Jas. 5. 4 labourers who have reaped down your

4. *To reap, gather in the harvest,* θερίζω *therizō.*
   Matt. 6. 26 neither do they reap, nor gather into ba.
      25. 24 reaping where thou hast not sown, and
      25. 26 I reap where I sowed not, and gather wh.
   Luke 12. 24 they neither sow nor reap; which neither
      19. 21 thou..reapest that thou didst not sow
      19. 22 taking up..and reaping that
   John 4. 36 that reapeth receiveth wages, and ga.
      4. 36 he that soweth and he that reapeth may
      4. 37 saying true, One soweth, and another re.
      4. 38 I sent you to reap that whereon ye best.
   1 Co. 9. 11 a great thing if we shall reap your carnal
   2 Co. 9. 6 He which soweth sparingly shall reap also
      9. 6 he which soweth bountifully shall reap
   Gal. 6. 7 whatsoever a man soweth..shall he alsor.
      6. 8 For he..shall of the flesh reap corruption
      6. 8 he..shall of the spirit reap life everlasting
      6. 9 in due season we shall reap, if we faint
   Jas. 5. 4 cries of them which have reaped are en.
   Rev. 14. 15 Thrust in thy sickle and reap: for the time
      14. 15 is come for thee to reap; for the harvest
      14. 16 thrust in his sickle..and the earth was r.

REAPER, REAPING —
1. *To shorten, reap,* קָצַר *qatsar.*
   Ruth 2. 3 gleaned in the field after the reapers: and
      2. 4 said unto the reapers, The LORD (be) with
      2. 5, 6 servant that was set over the reapers
      2. 7 let me glean and gather after the reapers
      2. 14 she sat beside the reapers: and he reached
   1 Sa. 6. 13 reaping their wheat harvest in the valley
   2 Ki. 4. 18 he went out to his father to the reapers
   Amos 9. 13 that the plowman shall overtake the re.
2. *A reaper,* θεριστής *theristēs.*
   Matt 13. 30 I will say to the reapers, Gather ye toge.
      13. 39 is the end of the world; and the reapers

2. Study how the word is used in the verse or passage. From the list of references in the concordance, choose the verse or passage you think best represents the meaning of the word. Write an initial proposal about the meaning of the word as it is used in the primary verse or passage you have chosen. You can refine your proposal after you work through the broader circles of context.

3. Study the use of the word in the same book. How is your word used in a particular book of the Bible? Find every place in the book where the author uses the Greek or Hebrew word you are studying. Look in a concordance for every reference of that Greek or Hebrew root word listed from the book you are studying. If you do not know what the Greek or Hebrew word is, trace the English word through the book. Look up each verse and note all of the different meanings of the word. Under each different meaning you find, list the references of the verses in which the word has that meaning.

4. Study the use of the word by the same author. This step is essentially the same as that just completed, except now you are listing all of the verses where the same author uses the word. You will need to examine all of the verses listed for the author's writings and find those which use the same Greek or Hebrew word you are studying. Once you've found the verses, organize them according to meaning.

5. Study the use of the word in either the Old or New Testament. Your goal here is to discover how other writers of Scripture used this word, first because they were contemporaries, but also because they were inspired by the same Holy Spirit. They may have used the same word in the same way. The procedure is the same as for the previous steps except that now you are using verse references for the whole Old or New Testament.

By this point in your study, you should have looked up every place in Scripture where your word occurs, and discovered its range of meanings. In essence, you've just completed the observation stage of your word study. Now it's time to decide (interpret) which meaning is correct in the verse you are studying.

Interpreting Word Studies
Here are four principles to help you decide which meaning of a word is the one the author most likely intended.

1. Some meanings will not fit and can be rejected immediately. Test each of the meanings you have uncovered to see which fits naturally and which clearly do not fit.

2. Some contexts are more important than others for determining what a word means in a specific section of Scripture. Generally, the meanings which are found in the same book are more likely to be the intended meaning than those used by the same author in other books. Likewise, meanings used by the same author are more likely to be the intended meaning than those used by other Old or New Testament authors. This principle is particularly true when the word tends to have a consistent meaning in the same book, or by the same author, or throughout the entire Old or New Testament.

3. Ultimately, the immediate context must be the final judge. It's possible that an author would use a word with the same meaning every time but that this meaning just does not fit the verse you are studying. If another meaning makes more sense in the context, it should be accepted. It is helpful to look at how the word is related to other words in the sentence and surrounding sentences. Does it modify any other words? Do other words modify it? Is it compared or contrasted with any other words? Be sure to look for parallelisms, especially in poetic literature. Your goal is to see if one meaning is more appropriate to these word relationships than other meanings. (For example, 1 Timothy 2:15 uses the Greek word *sozo*. This word normally means either "spiritual salvation" or "physical salvation from danger." In this context, however, the word is used to describe something that happens to women through the process of childbearing. The context forces most commentators to look for another meaning of *sozo* in this verse.)

4. Check your results with secondary sources. Though the process described above is sufficient for most word studies you will do, other resources can be considered. For instance, you could explore the meaning of the word *sozo* in the Septuagint (the Greek Old Testament) or the use of similar words in related languages like Accadian or Aramaic. These, however, are beyond the reach of most people, since many of us lack the linguistic training to explore such circles of context.

Applying Word Studies

The same four suggestions we've used before to apply Scripture to life apply also to word studies:

1. Know yourself. What needs in your own life stand out as you are studying the word?

2. Relate the word to life. In light of the series of new relationships (p. 75), what specific application principles come to mind as you think of the *word* you are studying?

3. Meditate on the results. Concentrate on finding one key verse as you study. Then think about what it says throughout the day and ask God to make it a part of your life.

4. Practice your findings. Ask yourself, "How can I respond based on what I've learned?" Then write down a specific action to take.

Observe Interpret Apply

YOUR TURN

Select one of the words below and use as many of the techniques from this chapter as you think appropriate to discover its meaning.

- ☐ the word "head" in Ephesians 5:23
- ☐ the word "virgin" in Isaiah 7:14
- ☐ the word "day" in Genesis 1:5

CHAPTER 19
How to Study a Doctrine

Theology and doctrine summarize what we believe, and what we believe is crucial to our experience of God. In most ways, we study doctrine in the same way as any other biblical topic. But this chapter will suggest additional study techniques to help you adopt doctrinal beliefs that are truly biblical. We sometimes think of doctrine as a potentially divisive topic best suited to people in academia. Yet Scripture assures us that sound teaching (doctrine) is the responsibility of all believers.

> *But in your hearts set apart Christ as Lord. Always be prepared to give an answer to everyone who asks you to give the reason for the hope that you have. But do this with gentleness and respect.*
> —*1 Peter 3:15*

Part of our calling as Christians is to know how to handle the Word of God and His truths accurately. Notice how Paul emphasized sound doctrine as an essential criteria for being a church leader:

> *If you point these things out to the brothers, you will be a good minister of Christ Jesus, brought up in the truths of the faith and of the good teaching that you have followed. . . . Until I come, devote yourself to the public reading of Scripture, to preaching and to teaching. . . . Be diligent in these matters; give yourself wholly to them, so that everyone may see your progress.*
> —*1 Timothy 4:6, 13, 15*

Observe Interpret Apply

Do your best to present yourself to God as one approved, a workman who does not need to be ashamed and who correctly handles the word of truth.
— 2 Timothy 2:15

Preach the Word; be prepared in season and out of season; correct, rebuke and encourage — with great patience and careful instruction. For the time will come when men will not put up with sound doctrine. Instead, to suit their own desires, they will gather around them a great number of teachers to say what their itching ears want to hear.
— 2 Timothy 4:2-3

There are several ways to study doctrines in Scripture. You can study particular words (*grace, justification, sanctification, sin, love, truth*), or a theological idea (the attributes of God). The same procedure applies to both types of study.

Observing a Doctrine
The following is a list of major areas of theological consideration. This list will give you some idea of the possible areas of doctrinal or theological study.

POSSIBLE AREAS OF THEOLOGY

Bibliology:	the study of the origin of the Bible.
Theology Proper:	the study of God's triune personality — (His attributes, divine works, names, trinity)
Angelology:	the study of angels (including Satan)
Anthropology:	the study of the origin and nature of man
Soteriology:	the study of salvation
Ecclesiology:	the study of the church
Eschatology:	the study of future things
Christology:	the study of the person of Christ
Pneumatology:	the study of the Holy Spirit

When doing a theological study, begin with these six steps:

1. Select the subject. A quick look at the table of contents in a systematic theology textbook will give you loads of ideas for study.

How to Study a Doctrine

2. Gather all the data. In doing a doctrinal study, follow the same basic approach you would for other topical studies, gathering all the important information you can on that particular doctrine. If you wanted to study the doctrine of eternity, you would look up *eternity* in a concordance to find where that word occurs. Using those cross-references, you would try to isolate the most significant passages on that doctrine.

3. Organize your findings. Organize your findings into a logical presentation. To do this, ask yourself:

- ☐ *What are the key words?* There are probably a number of words that relate to the doctrine you are studying. Make a list of all those different words with Scripture references.

- ☐ *What key books or passages teach this doctrine?* Some sections of the Bible teach certain doctrines more explicitly or implicitly than others. Make a note of where to find teachings on certain doctrinal issues in the Bible.

- ☐ *What problems does this doctrine raise?* Do people have misconceptions or problems with the particular doctrine you've chosen to study? List some of the problems or questions people have in relation to the doctrine.

- ☐ *Is the doctrine traced from the Old Testament to the New?* Notice whether or not the doctrine is progressive in its revelation: as you move through Scripture, does there seem to be more information that adds to your understanding of the doctrine?

- ☐ *Did Jesus teach or mention this doctrine?* Look up the occurrences of the doctrinal word you are studying to see if it is found in Christ's teachings in the Gospels. Note what Christ taught or implied about the doctrine.

- ☐ *Does the information correct any false views you are aware of on this doctrine?* Scripture warns us to beware of false teachers who would corrupt the truth. Many heresies started out as correct. Overemphasizing certain aspects of a doctrine can corrupt the doctrine. What false teachings have emerged from the doctrine you are studying? State them and try to list some of the truths you have found which correct those false teachings.

4. State the doctrine carefully. Now state the results of your study carefully and concisely. Can you do it in one or two sentences? Try to express the teachings of the doctrine simply and succinctly.

5. Consult secondary sources. What do other books about biblical doctrine add to your understanding of the one you are studying? In one sense, theological study is best left to skilled theologians. Doctrine and theology are woven throughout the pages of Scripture and are not easily identified or analyzed. Read what theologians or commentators say about the doctrine under consideration. Make a note of their thinking. In the event that you have opportunity to teach or preach the material you've researched, it's always helpful to have supporting material from other recognized authorities. Their comments can help make sure your conclusions are on target.

6. Choose a primary passage. Try to focus on one or two key passages of Scripture that teach the doctrine you are studying. Note several of the most important Scriptures for future reference.

Interpreting Doctrines

1. State the doctrine carefully. Refer to your observations of the doctrine and summarize what you've learned about it up to this point. Crystallize the teachings you've discovered about the particular doctrine you're studying.

2. State the teaching principles. Make a list of the various teachings you have found through your study that apply to Christian living. State these teachings as concise, brief principles.

3. Survey/consult the secondary sources. What did study aids add to your understanding of the doctrine?

4. State your conclusions. Write a concluding statement of interpretation based on your final thoughts and study. This statement should summarize the main teachings of the doctrine.

Applying Doctrines

Concerning how to apply doctrinal studies, use the same four suggested steps you have practiced throughout this book.

1. Know yourself. What needs in your own life stand out as you are studying this doctrine?

2. Relate the doctrine to life. In light of the series of new relationships (p. 75), what specific application principles come to mind as you think of the doctrine you are studying?

3. Meditate on the results. Concentrate on finding one key verse as you study. Then, throughout the day, think about what it says. Ask God to make it a part of your life.

How to Study a Doctrine

4. Practice your findings. Ask yourself, "Based on what I've learned, how can I respond?" Then write down a specific action to take.

YOUR TURN

Select a biblical doctrine: sanctification, the deity of Christ, eternal life, or some other doctrine that interests you. Using the techniques described here and in chapter 16, do some preliminary research on your topic making notes below. Then outline what you would do if you were to continue to study that doctrine in depth.

PERSONAL EVALUATION

When you began this workbook you came with certain expectations and goals. Some of them you were aware of and others were perhaps more unconscious. We've covered a lot of material in this workbook on inductive Bible study. Referring back to the goals you defined for yourself at the beginning (p. 12), how well did it meet your expectations for learning?

Goals Achieved:

Make a list of the goals you achieved in working through this book. Note anything that was particularly meaningful or helpful about these achievements—even if the goal was not something that occurred to you when you were making your notes on page 12.

Personal Evaluation

Goals to be Achieved:

Write down any personal study goals that remain to be attained. Why are they important to you? What can you do to meet these goals in the future?

Now that you have completed this workbook don't just assign it a place on your shelf. This book was designed to be a workbook *and* a reference text. Here are some practical suggestions for continuing to use this book in the future:

- ☐ *Keep a Bible study notebook.* Most of your work has been done in this workbook, so you will not have room to record future study projects here. Create a notebook of your own, following the same outlines that you've used here.

- ☐ *Review this workbook periodically.* You will probably find it helpful to refresh your memory on certain parts of this book. Repetition will help you to own for yourself the information presented here.

- ☐ *Study the workbook with a group.* If you have already been working through this book with a group, you may want to consider leading a group yourself next time. If you did the work by yourself, perhaps the insights of a group would bring up items you hadn't thought of on your own.

Build on the Rock

As Jesus drew His Sermon on the Mount to a close, He challenged His listeners to act on what they were hearing. He used the example of two men who built their houses on different foundations: one on the sand, the other on a rock. You know the story.

> *Therefore everyone who hears these words of mine and puts them into practice is like a wise man who built his house on the rock.*
> —*Matthew 7:24*

May you always build on the Rock.

GROUP STUDY GUIDE

General Guidelines for Leaders

Plan ahead. Before meeting with your group, read and study the chapter or chapters as if you were preparing for personal study. Glance through the questions, making notes of how you might contribute to the group's discussion. Bring a Bible and the workbook to each meeting.

Arrange an environment that promotes discussion. Comfortable chairs arranged in a casual circle invite people to talk with each other. Be sure to sit where you can have eye contact with each person.

Promptness counts. Time is valuable. If the group runs late (because of a late start), some people will feel frustrated. Unless you have a mutual agreement, begin and end on time.

Involve everyone. Group learning works best if everyone participates more or less equally. If you are a natural *talker,* pause before you enter the conversation. Then ask a quiet person what he or she thinks. If you are a natural *listener* don't hesitate to jump into the discussion. Others will benefit from your thoughts. As the leader, be careful not to dominate the discussion. You will be well prepared to answer the questions, but people are not there to hear you. Help the group members to make their own discoveries. Try to avoid tangents by bringing attention of the group back to the focus of that meeting. Ask the questions listed and insert your own ideas only as they are needed to fill gaps.

Pace the study. The questions for each study are designed to last about one hour. The first few questions provide the framework for the rest of the questions, so don't rush through them. It is your responsibility to time the flow of questions.

Pray for each other—together and alone. Watch how God works in the lives of people in your group as you practice studying Scripture together.

GROUP STUDY #1
For Chapters 1 and 2

Leader Preparation: The focus of this first session is twofold. (1) To gain an appreciation for the unique nature of Scripture: its divine inspiration gives it the authority to teach, correct, and train (2 Timothy 3:16-17). (2) To become familiar with the three steps of inductive Bible study. Read each question out loud and have the group discuss it.

Group Participation

1. What are some ways the Bible is unique from any other book?

2. Since the Bible is unique, how does this change the way we read and study Scripture?

3. Why did God give us the Scriptures? Try first to answer the question on your own and then read 2 Timothy 3:16-17.

4. How has the message of 2 Timothy 3:16-17 been true for your life?

5. What are some reasons why we actually need to *work* at understanding the Bible—that it doesn't always come easily?

6. Share an experience (it could be positive or negative) about Bible study requiring hard work. What did you learn from the experience?

7. List some of the benefits that come from studying Scripture. Which ones have been especially true for you.

8. Share one of your personal goals for working through this book (see p. 12). Explain why this goal is important to you?

9. What are the three steps of inductive Bible study, and why is each step important in the study of Scripture?

10. Turn in the book to the exercise on Jonah 1 on pp. 16–17. Go around the group and share your answers to each of the four questions.

New Insights
☐ Take five minutes and record below any new insights you have gained through the discussion time.

☐ Write one specific way you can begin to apply one of these insights so that you love God and others more faithfully. Share your application with the group.

GROUP STUDY #2
For Chapters 3 through 6

Leader Preparation: In this session, try to help the group to appreciate each stage of observing a passage or book of the Bible. Keep coming back to the example given in the fish story as an illustration of how to do thorough observation of Scripture.

Group Participation

1. We began our study of how to observe Scripture with the Fish Story. How would you describe the central message of that story?

2. When have you been in a similar situation as the student, where you were forced to keep plugging away at a project only to find in the end that you were the better for it?

3. What did you learn from the fish story that you can apply to observing a passage of Scripture?

4. What are the three stages of *observation?* Why is each stage an important part of observing a passage or book of the Bible? (If you need help, turn to page 26.)

5. How could you be practicing the three stages of observation in your own life (perhaps in a situation at work or a relationship)?

6. What are the four questions of observation? Name a few of the items covered in each category, then refer to the answers on p. 31.

7. In observing the *who, what, where,* and *when* of Philippians 2:1-11, which question did you find most difficult to answer? Why was it difficult?

8. Having observed the whole, the parts, and the details of Philippians 2:1-11, what did you notice that you had not seen before? What impact does your insight have on future Bible studies? On your relationship with Christ?

9. Chapter 6 begins with the advertisement about "How to Read a Love Letter." What are some reasons why we read a love letter differently than we read the newspaper?

10. In a sense, the Bible is God's love letter to us; through Scripture God communicates His heart for us. What are some ways you can cultivate in your life this perspective of God speaking to you personally through the Bible?

New Insights
☐ Take five minutes and record below any new insights you have gained through the discussion time.

☐ Write one specific way you can begin to apply one of these insights so that you love God and others more. Share your application with the group.

GROUP STUDY #3
For Chapters 7 and 8

Leader Preparation: This is perhaps the most difficult stage of Bible study. It's often easier to pick out the facts and make applications; it's a discipline to take the necessary time to determine *the author's intention* in writing. Keep coming back to the importance of this step as you discuss the questions below.

Group Participation

1. What are some ways (good or bad) that you have seen people interpret Scripture?

2. What is the definition of interpretation? Try to answer the question yourselves before referring to the information on pages 46–48.

3. The author uses the example of buying a car to illustrate how we often interpret facts without being aware of it in the course of making decisions. When have you experienced the process of interpretation in your everyday life?

4. Do you read a poem the same way you read the newspaper? Explain.

5. Describe the four principles that govern how we ought to interpret the Bible? Again, try to answer the question on your own before turning back in the book (p. 49). How can you commit these principles to memory?

6. When you study a book or passage of Scripture, why do you think it's important to first understand what the author was saying to his original audience?

Observe Interpret Apply

7. Try to name the five C's of interpretation, in order, from memory. (Check your memory with page 52.)

8. In your study of Philippians 2:1-11 in chapter 8, what was the hardest part about determining its meaning? Why was it difficult?

9. Now that you have gone through the process of interpretation once, what are some things you would do differently next time?

New Insights
☐ Take five minutes and record below any new insights you have gained through the discussion time.

☐ Write one specific way you can begin to apply one of these insights so that you love God and others more. Share your application with the group.

GROUP STUDY #4
For Chapters 9 and 10

Leader Preparation: These two chapters lay the groundwork for proper application. Remind the group that more specific guidelines are discussed in Part Two. As you discuss how to apply the Bible, be sure their suggested actions are as specific, personal, and attainable as possible.

Group Participation

1. What is *application?*

2. Why is application so important? Is there such a thing as understanding that produces no change in a person's life? Explain your answer.

3. Name some Bible characters (both Old and New Testament) who failed to apply what they knew of God's Word—as well as some who did. What were some of the results in both cases?

4. Share an example of how you have applied a Bible passage to your life. How did you benefit from your obedience?

5. Share your answers to the exercise concerning whether the passages given apply directly to you or not (pp. 68–69). Summarize some of the group's reasons for applying or not directly applying a text to our lives.

6. What are three questions that need to be answered before we can apply a passage to our lives? After answering this question, read together the summary principle on page 70 and discuss any questions you have about it.

Observe Interpret Apply

7. How does the Bible limit its own application? What are some examples where people have not followed these limitations?

8. Having worked through these chapters on application, you may have noticed an area in your life where you believe God wants you to apply His Word in a more personal, obedient way. What is one area, and what specific action can you take to obey God more fully?

9. Of the four general guidelines for applying Scripture, which is the hardest for you and why? (If necessary, refresh your memory by looking at page 72.)

10. Have two or three people share one of their application questions from page 71 and see if the group can be of help.

New Insights
☐ Take five minutes and record below any new insights you have gained through the discussion time.

☐ Write one specific way you can begin to apply one of these insights so that you love God and others more. Share your application with the group.

GROUP STUDY #5
For Chapters 11 and 12

Leader Preparation: Help the group to thoroughly cover the material in chapter 12, allowing time for people to ask any general questions about studying whole books (ch. 11) or specific questions concerning narratives. Since this is the first time they have applied the inductive approach to a whole book, encourage them to learn from each other.

Group Participation

1. What is your favorite type of biblical literature? Why?

2. Name three books in each literary category: narrative, epistle, wisdom literature, poetry, and prophecy.

3. How would you describe *narrative* literature?

4. Turn back to Fee and Stuart's list of four things narratives are *not* (p. 86). Which one did you find most interesting and helpful? Why?

5. This is the first time you have had the chance to apply the three steps of inductive Bible study to a whole book. What questions or difficulties did you encounter as you observed the Gospel of John?

6. Take a few minutes to share your book charts for the Gospel of John (pp. 97–99). How does your chart compare with the others in your group? Share one insight you gained from the process of charting the Book of John.

7. Go around the group and have each read aloud one of the principles for interpreting narratives from page 100. Pause after reading each one for observations and discussion.

8. All narrative books of the Bible address the same *need*. What is that need? (If necessary, review the material on page 101.)

   Given that need, why do you suppose God chose to use so much of this type of literature in Scripture?

9. What did you conclude is the message of the Gospel of John (p. 104)? How was your conclusion shaped by following the previous steps of interpretation?

10. Share one of your principles for applying the Gospel of John to your life (p. 106). Have two or three people share how they have decided to specifically work on one of their applications this week.

New Insights
☐ Take five minutes and record below any new insights you have gained through the discussion time.

☐ Write one specific way you can begin to apply one of these insights so that you love God and others more. Share your application with the group.

GROUP STUDY #6
For Chapter 13

Leader Preparation: Help the group to grasp the unique nature of epistles by reminding them throughout the discussion time of the example of how we read personal letters (question 1). This genre is perhaps the most misused type of biblical literature, so make sure the group is clear on what epistles are and the particular rules that govern their interpretation and application.

Group Participation

1. Think of a time you received a letter from someone you love. What did you do?

2. What is an epistle? How is it different from a narrative? How is it similar?

3. From your study of 1 Thessalonians, what questions or comments do you have about observing epistles? About making a book chart for them?

4. What did you learn about interpreting epistles that was new to you? How is this concept/caution/principle helpful for understanding this kind of literature?

5. Share your initial proposal for the need and message of 1 Thessalonians (p. 124). How did you revise you answers later (p. 125)?

6. The chapter begins with two examples of how *not* to apply epistles (p. 107). Have two or three people share other examples from their own experience. (You will discuss the reasons for these misapplications in the next question.)

7. Discuss the general principles for applying epistles (p. 126). What questions or observations do you have about these guidelines?

Review the flawed applications that came out of your discussion of question 6. How might following one of these principles have prevented that mistake?

8. Did you find it easy or difficult to write five applications for 1 Thessalonians? Why?

9. What action did you purpose to take this week based on what you learned from your study of 1 Thessalonians?

New Insights
☐ Take five minutes and record below any new insights you have gained through the discussion time.

☐ Write one specific way you can begin to apply one of these insights so that you love God and others more. Share your application with the group.

GROUP STUDY #7
For Chapter 14

Leader Preparation: The wisdom and poetic literature of the Bible often hold a special place in people's hearts. Help your group to make personal connections between the colorful language and rich imagery the writers used and their own communication with God.

Group Participation

1. Share one way you have used the wisdom or poetic books of Scripture.

2. Name all five of the wisdom and poetic books. Which one are you most familiar with and why?

3. When the Bible speaks of *wisdom* what does it mean? What are some examples from Scripture of this kind of wisdom? The lack of wisdom?

4. Referring to the literary devices listed on pages 129–131, what questions do you have about these devices or the examples given?

5. Why do you think God has chosen to use such a variety of forms to communicate His Word to us? How would you support your answer from Scripture?

6. The special features of poetry listed on pages 143–144 give background knowledge for studying Psalms and Song of Solomon. Take a moment to go through this material and discuss any questions or observations the group has.

Observe Interpret Apply

7. Go around the group and share your answers to the observation exercise on Job (pp.134–135). Compare your final chart of the Book of Job with those of the others in the group.

8. As you went through the steps for interpreting Job (pages 139–141), what did you learn that was new to you? Which secondary resource was particularly helpful to you and why?

9. Taking into account all of your study of Job, how would you answer the question: *Why did Job repent?*

10. How did you decide to apply the message of Job in your life this week?

11. Select a favorite passage from the closing chapters of Job. Give each person a chance to read his or her favorite lines and explain their personal significance.

New Insights
☐ Take five minutes and record below any new insights you have gained through the discussion time.

☐ Write one specific way you can begin to apply one of these insights so that you love God and others more. Share your application with the group.

GROUP STUDY #8
For Chapter 15

Leader Preparation: There are many misconceptions about interpreting and applying prophetic literature, so it may be tempting to get on tangents in this study. Be familiar with all the material presented in this chapter and allow time to cover each of the discussion questions.

Group Participation

1. What is the most outrageous interpretation of biblical prophecy you've ever heard?

2. According to Scripture, what is a prophet? What are the names of some of the major prophets? Some minor prophets?

3. Why is the Book of Revelation included in this category of literature? In what ways is it similar to the Old Testament books? How is it different?

4. Why do you think the author took care to note the historical nature of the prophetic books, as well as some words of caution in understanding them?

5. You had a chance to practice studying a prophetic book by looking at Micah. Compare with each other your observations of this book (pp. 165–168), and ask any questions you have about the process.

6. What are the four events to which the prophets pointed? (Refer to the answers on page 169 only after trying to name them on your own.)

Observe Interpret Apply

7. Of the four main ways of interpreting the Book of Revelation (p. 169), which school of thought most reflects your own? Why?

8. How do you think that your perspective on Revelation influences the way you view the questions of *who, what, where, when,* and *why?*

9. What would you say to someone who said to you: "I don't read the prophetic books because they talk about people or things that I don't understand or that don't apply to me"?

10. How has this chapter on prophetic books affected the way you view this type of biblical literature?

New Insights
☐ Take five minutes and record below any new insights you have gained through the discussion time.

☐ Write one specific way you can begin to apply one of these insights so that you love God and others more. Share your application with the group.

GROUP STUDY #9
For Chapters 16 through 19

Leader Preparation: There is a great deal of information given in these last chapters, so budget enough time to be able to discuss all the questions and still leave time at the end to pray for one another.

Group Participation

1. If you had the chance to study any topic, person, word, or theological doctrine, what would you choose and why?

2. What are some reasons why topical Bible studies are so popular? Evaluate the merit of the reasons people choose topical studies.

3. The author notes that we study certain topics, people, words, or doctrines in some books and not in others (pp. 178–179). If you wanted to do a study on friendship what books, people, words would you look up? Share some of your reasons why.

4. Because the steps for studying topics are slightly different from what you have studied so far, you were asked to write any questions you had about observing them (p. 184). Now that you've had a chance to practice the steps, what questions do you still have?

5. Go around the group and have two people share their answers to each of the five observation steps on pages 187–191.

6. What teaching principles did you glean from your study of this topic?

Observe Interpret Apply

7. How can you respond to these principles based on what you have learned in this topical study?

8. Explain to the group something that you found particularly interesting in your personal study of chapters 17–19. (See pages 198, 203, and 290).

9. Share your answers to the Personal Evaluation sheet on pages 210–211.

New Insights
☐ Take five minutes and record below any new insights you have gained through the discussion time.

☐ Take a few minutes to thank God for the tools you've learned in studying Scripture. In view of the goals you shared (question 9), pray for each other's continued use of what you have learned. Ask God to grow you in wisdom, understanding, and godly character, as you apply these tools in your future study of God's Word.

APPENDIX A
Defining Bible Study Aids

Here is a list of resources that make a good Bible study library. They are books or software programs that you will want to consult during the interpretation stage of your study.

Bible Atlas: Maps with commentary.

Bible dictionary/encyclopedia: These are often the single most valuable tool to use. Bible dictionaries contain words in alphabetical order with information about their usage. Bible encyclopedias contain alphabetical information on the branches of knowledge related to the Bible.

Commentary: This resource provides an explanation of the meaning of individual and collective passages of Scripture. Commentaries vary in their length, depth of detail, and how closely they stick to the words of Scripture.

Concordance: This is an exhaustive alphabetical list of every word in the Bible and every instance where that word is used. Each Bible translation (such as *The New International Version* (NIV), *The New Revised Standard Version* (NRSV), or *The New American Standard Bible* (NASB), has its own corresponding concordance. This resource allows you to see how a word is used in more than just one context, thereby yielding a fuller understanding of a word.

Lexicon: A dictionary explaining the meaning of biblical words listed in the original languages: Greek, Hebrew, and/or Aramaic.

Word study: A book showing one person's determination of the meaning of words in their various uses throughout Scripture.

APPENDIX B
Bible Study Resource List

Bible Atlases

Aharoni, Yohanan, et al., eds. *The Macmillan Bible Atlas.* 3rd ed. New York: Macmillan, 1993.

May, Herbert G., ed. *Oxford Bible Atlas.* 3rd ed. Oxford: Oxford University Press, 1985.

Pfeiffer, Charles F., ed. *Baker's Bible Atlas.* Rev. ed. Grand Rapids: Baker, 1961.

Bible Dictionaries/Encyclopedias

Bromiley, Geoffrey W., ed., *The International Standard Bible Encyclopedia.* Rev. ed. 4 vols. Grand Rapids: Eerdmans, 1979–88.

Douglas, James D., ed. *The New Bible Dictionary.* 2d ed. Wheaton: Tyndale, 1982.

Elwell, Walter A. *Evangelical Dictionary of Theology.* Grand Rapids: Baker, 1984.

Harrison, Everett, ed. *Baker's Dictionary of Theology.* Grand Rapids: Baker, 1960.

Tenney, Merrill C., ed. *The Zondervan Pictorial Encyclopedia of the Bible.* 5 vols. Grand Rapids: Zondervan, 1975.

Commentaries

(For an overall guide to choosing between commentaries see Stuart, Douglas. *A Guide to Selecting and Using Bible Commentaries.* Dallas: Word, 1990.)

Guthrie, Donald, et al., eds. *New Bible Commentary.* Grand Rapids: Eerdmans, 1987.

Ironside, H.A. *James and Peter.* Neptune, N.J.: Loizeaux Brothers, Inc., 1947.

Unger, Merrill F. *Unger's Bible Handbook.* Chicago: Moody, 1988.

Walvoord, John and Roy B. Zuck. *Bible Knowledge Commentary: Old Testament and New Testament.* Wheaton: Victor Books, 1983.

Walvoord, John. *Philippians.* Chicago: Moody, 1971.

Wiseman, D.J., ed. *The Tyndale Old Testament Commentaries.* Leicester, England and Downers Grove, Illinois: InterVarsity, 1964–1993.

Concordances

(Refer to a concordance that corresponds with your Bible translation.)

Old Testament:

Wigram, George V. *The Englishman's Hebrew and Chaldee Concordance of the Old Testament.* Reprint. Grand Rapids: Zondervan, 1980.

Appendix B

New Testament:

Mouton, William F., et al. *A Concordance to the Greek Testament*. 5th ed. Edinburgh: T & T Clark, 1978.

Strong, James. *Strong's Exhaustive Concordance of the Bible*. Peabody, MA: Hendrickson, 1988.

Young, Robert. *Young's Analytical Concordance of the Bible*. Peabody, MA: Hendrickson.

Lexicons

Holladay, William L. *A Concise Hebrew and Aramaic Lexicon of the Old Testament*. Grand Rapids: Eerdmans, 1972.

Bauer, Walter, et al., eds. *A Greek-English Lexicon of the New Testament and Other Early Christian Literature*. Trans. William F. Arndt. Chicago: University of Chicago Press, 1979.

Software

Hermeneutika Bible Research Software, P.O. Box 98563, Seattle, WA 98198.

Logos Bible Software, Logos Research Systems, 2117 200th Avenue West, Oak Harbor, WA 98277.

PC Study Bible, BibleSoft, 22014 7th Avenue So., Seattle, WA 98198.

Quick Verse and PC Bible Atlas, Parson's Technology, One Parsons Drive, Hiawatha, IA 52233

Word Search Computer Bible, NavPress Software, P.O. Box 6000, Colorado Springs, CO 80934.

Word Studies

Nave, Orville J. *Nave's Topical Bible*. Chicago: Moody, 1976.

Harris, R. Laird, et al., eds. *Theological Wordbook of the Old Testament*. 2 vols. Chicago: Moody, 1980.

Brown, Colin, ed. *The New International Dictionary of New Testament Theology*. 3 vols. Grand Rapids: Zondervan, 1975.

Miscellaneous

Bright, John. *A History of Israel*. 3d ed. Louisville, KY: Westminster/John Knox, 1981.

Carson, D.A. *Exegetical Fallacies*. Grand Rapids: Baker, 1984.

Fee, Gordon D. and Douglas Stuart. *How to Read the Bible for All It's Worth*. Grand Rapids: Zondervan, 1981.

Inch, Morris A. and C. Hassell Bullock. *The Literature and Meaning of Scripture*. Grand Rapids: Baker, 1981.

Jensen, Irving, *Jensen's Bible Study Charts* 2 vols. Chicago: Moody, 1981.

Jensen, Irving. *Independent Bible Study*. Chicago: Moody, 1963.

Kuhatschek, Jack. *Taking the Guesswork out of Applying the Bible*. Downers Grove, Ill.: InterVarsity Press, 1990.

McQuilken, J. Robertson. *Understanding and Applying the Bible*. Chicago: Moody, 1983.

Mears, Henrietta C. *What the Bible Is All About*. Rev. ed. Wheaton: Tyndale, 1987.

Ryken, Leland. *The Literature of the Bible*. Grand Rapids: Zondervan, 1974.

Traina, Robert. *Methodical Bible Study*. Wilmore, KY: Robert Traina, 1952.

APPENDIX C
Principles of Structure

COMPARISON: the association of like things.

The Word of God is compared to a sword that is sharp and pierces people's consciences:

> *For the word of God is living and active. Sharper than any double-edged sword, it penetrates even to dividing soul and spirit, joints and marrow; it judges the thoughts and attitudes of the heart.*
>
> *—Hebrews 4:12*

CONTRAST: the association of things which are opposite.

Psalm 1 is based on this structural device. The righteous man (vv. 1-3) is contrasted with the unrighteous man (vv. 4-6).

In 1 Thessalonians 5:4-10 the "sons of light" (Christians) are contrasted with "the sons of darkness" (unbelievers):

> *But you, brothers, are not in darkness so that this day should surprise you like a thief. You are all sons of the light and sons of the day. We do not belong to the night or to the darkness. So then, let us not be like others, who are asleep, but let us be alert and self-controlled. For those who sleep, sleep at night, and those who get drunk, get drunk at night. But since we belong to the day, let us be self-controlled, putting on faith and love as a breastplate, and the hope of salvation as a helmet. For God did not appoint us to suffer wrath but to receive salvation through our Lord Jesus Christ. He died for us so that, whether we are awake or asleep, we may live together with Him.*

REPETITION: the reiteration of the same or similar terms, phrases, clauses, or concepts.

In Ephesians 1, note the repetition of the phrases: *in Christ, through Christ, in Him* and similar phrases (1:3), *in Him* (1:4), *through Jesus Christ* (1:5), *in the one He loves* (1:6), *in Him* (1:7), *in Christ* (1:9), *under Christ* (1:10), *in Him* (1:11), *in Christ* (1:12), *in Christ* (1:13). By using repetition, Paul makes it clear that all of our spiritual blessings are because of Jesus Christ and His work on our behalf.

Another example is in the Book of Acts where the phrase "signs and wonders" is repeated (see Acts 2:22, 43; 4:30; 5:12; 6:8; 7:36; 14:3; 15:12). Luke uses repetition to impress on his readers that through the church, Jesus Christ continues His ministry on the earth. The ascended Christ who has received all power in heaven and on earth continues to testify to the work of salvation which God achieved through Him by performing mighty "signs and wonders" through His disciples.

CAUSE TO EFFECT: the statement of a cause and then its effects.

In Galatians 6:7-8 the causes are "sowing to one's flesh or sowing to the Spirit," and the resulting effects are stated to be "corruption" and "eternal life."

Do not be deceived: God cannot be mocked. A man reaps what he sows. The one who sows to please his sinful nature, from that nature will reap destruction; the one who sows to please the Spirit, from the Spirit will reap eternal life.

The Books of 1 and 2 Kings also are structured around this device. These books describe Israel's idolatries and immoralities, as well as their resistance to God's gracious attempts to bring them to repentance through the ministries of prophets like Elijah and Elisha. The books are essentially a catalog of causes which build up to effects: the Assyrian and Babylonian captivities.

EFFECT TO CAUSE: the opposite of cause to effect; the statement or description of the effect(s) and then their cause(s).

Romans 8:22-30 is an example of this structural device. Paul first states the "effect" in verses 22-27 where he describes the believer's eager longing for the redemption of the body and his unshakable hope, even in the face of suffering (v. 18). Paul then states the *cause* of this attitude in verses 28-30 where he describes the assurance all believers have that "all things work together for good," and the certainty of the Christian's eventual glorification at Christ's return.

EXPLANATION: the introduction of an idea which is then expanded or explained.

Mark 4:3-9 and verses 10-20 are an example of this structural device. First, Jesus tells the Parable of the Sower in verses 3-9. This is followed by Jesus' explanation of the parable in verses 10-20.

ILLUSTRATION: the introduction of an idea, followed by an illustration (example) of it.

Hebrews 11 uses this structural device. First the idea is presented in verses 1 and 2, "Now faith is being sure of what we hope for and certain of what we do not see. This is what the ancients were commended for." This idea is then illustrated throughout the rest of the chapter by the stories of Old Testament saints whose faith enabled them to accomplish mighty things for God and to gain His commendation.

The Book of Judges also uses this device. The author's purpose is to show how Israel's failure to obey God and drive the pagan nations out of Canaan resulted in compromise and moral depravity. Chapters 1–16 narrate the "cycles" of judges. Chapters 17–20 tell the stories of the idolatrous Danites and the molestation of the Levites' concubine by the Benjamites. These two stories are included at the end to illustrate the depths of Israel's depravity.

CLIMAX: the arrangement of the text in such a way that it progresses from the lesser to the greater (i.e., the story or discourse builds to a climax).

Paul uses this device in Romans. In the first eleven chapters he discusses several crucial theological truths: the sinfulness of all people and salvation by grace apart from the Law or works. Though some Christians today take these truths for granted, to the people of Paul's day they were strange and difficult to accept—especially for the Jews. One can imagine the original readers of this epistle becoming increasingly tense as they read through the letter until they came to Paul's exclamation in 11:33-36 beginning: "Oh, the depth of the riches of the wisdom and knowledge of God!" It is as if Paul is saying that even though these truths are difficult and we cannot completely understand them, rather than giving up in despair or skepticism, we should acknowledge that God's wisdom is beyond human understanding and we should respond in praise and reverence.

Another example of this structural principle is found in Exodus, which tells the story of Israel's deliverance from Egypt and God's decision to choose Israel to be an example to all nations. The story reaches its climax in Exodus 40:34-38 which relates how God, when the tabernacle was completed, filled it with His glory. This physical manifestation of His presence remained with Israel throughout their journeys.

PIVOT: the arrangement of subject matter so that there are pivotal points at which the story changes direction; pivots act like hinges in the text.

In 2 Samuel, chapters 11 and 12 are pivotal. The preceding chapters only describe David's conquests and his rapid rise to power. Chapters 11 and 12, however, relate David's sin with Bathsheba. After this point in the narrative, the whole tone of the narrative changes, as the focus shifts to a description of the tragic consequences of David's sin as seen in Absalom's rebellion (chs. 13–19), Sheba's rebellion (ch. 20), a famine (ch. 21), and finally, David's tragic mistake of numbering the people (ch. 24).

INTERCHANGE: the alternation or exchange of certain elements in the text; movement of the author back and forth between several ideas.

We see this structural principle in Luke 1–3, which weaves together the stories of John the Baptist and Jesus. The text moves back and forth between the two: the miraculous announcement of the birth of John (1:5-25), the miraculous announcement of the birth of

Jesus (1:26-56); the birth and early years of John (1:57-80), the birth and early years of Jesus (2:1-52). At 3:1-22 (the early ministry of John) the interchange ends. Once Jesus is baptized and God testified that He is His Son, Jesus' ministry grows and John's ministry fades; the greater replaces the lesser.

PREPARATION: the inclusion of background material or the setting for events or ideas to prepare the reader to understand that which follows.

Genesis 2 prepares the reader for Genesis 3 by describing the Garden of Eden, the creation of woman to be a helper for man, and the command not to eat the fruit of the tree of the knowledge of good and evil. Thus, when the Fall occurs (ch. 3), the reader better understands how sinful human rebellion really is; even though God had placed them in a perfect environment where all of their needs were met, man and woman were not satisfied and wanted the one thing God had forbidden them to have.

SUMMARY: the gathering together of main ideas by the author in order to clarify his thoughts; he seeks to express and then restate them in summary form.

Hebrews 8:1 is an example of this. In the first few chapters, the author of Hebrews describes the High Priestly ministry of Jesus Christ. Then in chapter 8, he begins to summarize by saying that the main point in what has been said is that we have a High Priest, who has taken His seat at the right hand of God, a minister in the true tabernacle which the Lord (not humanity) pitched. The author's point is that Christ, because He is a heavenly High Priest, is superior to any earthly high priest.

QUESTION POSED: the structuring of the text around questions which the author raises.

The Book of Romans uses this structural device where Paul leads his readers through his theological assertions by using questions. Each new question represents a change in the subject Paul is addressing. One can gain a good overview of the topics covered in Romans 2–11 simply by listing the questions Paul asks.

QUESTION ANSWERED: the structuring of the text around answers the author gives to a question, whether these questions are explicitly stated or merely implied.

First Corinthians 7 and 8 use this structural device. In chapter 7, Paul answers the Corinthians' questions about marriage. In chapter 8, Paul addresses another question about eating meat that has been sacrificed to idols. Evidently both of these were issues facing the Corinthian church, and Paul had been asked to give them authoritative answers. Note also that the specific questions are not stated in the text, but must be deduced from Paul's answers.

NOTES

Chapter 3:
1. Irving Jensen, *Independent Bible Study* (Chicago: Moody, 1963), 173–78. From *American Poems* (Boston: Houghton, Osgood, 1879), 450–54. This essay first appeared in *Every Saturday* (April 14, 1874), pp. 369–70, under the title "In the Laboratory with Agassiz, by a Former Pupil."

Chapter 7:
1. Irving Jensen, *Independent Bible Study* (Chicago: Moody, 1963), 73. Quoted by Edward Weeks, "The Peripatetic Reviewer," *The Atlantic Monthly*, vol. 185 (June 1950), p. 78. Attributed to Sir Ernest Gowers from the pamphlet "Plain Words."
2. Robert Traina, *Methodical Bible Study* (Wilmore, KY: Robert Traina, 1952), 94–95.
3. Jensen, 105, quoting Bernard Ramm, *Protestant Biblical Interpretation* (Grand Rapids: Baker, 1970), 105.

Chapter 8:
1. H.A. Ironside, *James and Peter* (Neptune, N.J.: Loizeaux Brothers, Inc., 1947), 9.
2. John Walvoord, *Philippians* (Chicago: Moody, 1971), 57–58.

Chapter 9:
1. Irving Jensen, *Independent Bible Study* (Chicago: Moody, 1963), preface.

Chapter 11:
1. Leland Ryken, *The Literature of the Bible* (Grand Rapids: Zondervan, 1974), 14–15.
2. Irving Jensen, *Independent Bible Study* (Chicago: Moody Press, 1963), 107.

Chapter 12:
1. Gordon D. Fee and Douglas Stuart, *How to Read the Bible for All It's Worth* (Grand Rapids: Zondervan, 1981), 75–77. Used by permission.
2. J. Robertson McQuilken, *Understanding and Applying the Bible* (Chicago: Moody, 1983), 241, 259.
3. Fee and Stuart, *How to Read the Bible for All It's Worth*, 78. Used by permission.
4. Leland Ryken, *The Literature of the Bible* (Grand Rapids: Zondervan, 1974), 275.

Chapter 13:
1. Merrill C. Tenney, ed., *Zondervan Pictorial Bible Dictionary* (Grand Rapids: Zondervan, 1975), 337.
2. Leland Ryken, *The Literature of the Bible* (Grand Rapids: Zondervan, 1974), 317.
3. See chap. 4 of Fee and Stuart's, *How to Read the Bible For All It's Worth*, for more information on how to interpret epistles.

Chapter 14:
1. Gordon D. Fee and Douglas Stuart, *How to Read the Bible for All It's Worth* (Grand Rapids: Zondervan, 1981), 187.
2. Ibid.

3. Ibid., 194–95.
4. Leland Ryken, *The Literature of the Bible* (Grand Rapids: Zondervan, 1974), 250–51. Used by permission.
5. Morris A. Inch and C. Hassell Bullock, *The Literature and Meaning of Scripture* (Grand Rapids: Baker, 1981), 65–66.
6. Ryken, *The Literature of the Bible*, 157.
7. Merrill F. Unger, *Unger's Bible Handbook* (Chicago: Moody, 1966), 274. Used by permission.

Chapter 15:
1. Gordon D. Fee and Douglas Stuart, *How to Read the Bible for All It's Worth* (Grand Rapids: Zondervan, 1981), 216.
2. Ibid., 149–50.
3. Ibid., 151.

Chapter 16:
1. Everett Harrison, ed. *Baker's Dictionary of Theology* (Grand Rapids: Baker, 1960), 538.

Observe Interpret Apply

SUMMARY

by Hans Finzel

Open my eyes that I may see wonderful things in Your Law.
—Psalm 119:18

THE INDUCTIVE APPROACH TO BIBLE STUDY

OBSERVATION — "What do I see?"
Observation moves from the general to the specific, investigating the facts in a passage.

A. Observe the Whole (getting an overview)

 1. Read the text carefully.
 2. Record your initial impressions.
 3. Record the major facts (who, what, where, and when).

B. Observe the Parts (finding the structure)

 1. Make a structural outline of the text.
 2. Mark the principles of structure in the text.

C. Observe the Details (looking at the major facts)

 1. Who?   The characters
 2. What?   The key truths or events
 3. Where?   The geography and location
 4. When?   The time factors

INTERPRETATION — "What does it mean?"
Interpretation is the science of discovering the author's original meaning as he wrote the Scriptures.

A. The Questions of Interpretation

 Ask further research questions of meaning concerning:

 1. Who?   The characters
 2. What?   The key truths or events
 3. Where?   The geography and location
 4. When?   The time factors
 5. Why?   The purpose of the text
    a. The reader's need
    b. The writer's message

B. The Answers for Interpretation

The questions of interpretation are answered by:

1. Stating an initial proposal
2. Studying the content
3. Searching the context
4. Seeking comparisons
5. Surveying secondary sources
6. Stating your conclusions

APPLICATION—"How should I respond?"
Application is action—learning how the truths discovered should affect your thoughts, feelings, and behavior, then diligently putting those truths to practice in your life.

A. Know yourself.

Look for applications in light of your own strengths and weaknesses.

B. Relate the passage to life.

1. Summarize truths that seem to apply to you.
2. Decide if they are timeless and universal.
3. Look for ways the text applies to new relationships.

C. Meditate on the passage.

Pick out one verse that summarizes how God is speaking to you through this passage, and memorize it.

D. Practice what you've learned.

Write down several action points to implement in your current situation.

Therefore everyone who hears these words of Mine,
and puts them into practice is like a wise man
who built his house on the rock
—Matthew 7:24.

© 1994 by Victor Books/SP Publications, Inc.